KING OF THE MOUNTAIN

KING OF THE MOUNTAIN

The story of Jerry Moore's rise from the depths of despair to lead the Appalachian State University Mountaineers to three straight national championships.

BY DICK BROWN

Published by DB Ink
Winston-Salem, North Carolina
Distributed to the trade by John F. Blair, Publisher

First Edition, 2008

Design by Angela Harwood

Printed in the United States

Library of Congress Cataloging-in-Publication Data

Brown, Dick, 1937 Dec. 21-
King of the mountain : the story of Jerry Moore's rise from the depths of despair to lead the Appalachian State University Mountaineers to three straight national championships / Dick Brown. -- 1st ed.
p. cm.
ISBN-13: 978-0-89587-367-5 (hardcover : alk. paper)
ISBN-10: 0-89587-367-2 (hardcover : alk. paper)
ISBN-13: 978-0-89587-368-2 (pbk. : alk. paper)
ISBN-10: 0-89587-368-0 (pbk. : alk. paper) 1. Moore, Jerry, 1939- 2. Football coaches--United States--Biography. 3. Appalachian State University--Football--Biography. 4. Appalachian State University Mountaineers (Football team)--Biography. I. Title.
GV939.M615B76 2008
796.332092--dc22
[B]
2008027588

"People may not remember who you are or what you say, but they will always remember how you made them feel."

Coach Jerry Moore, May 11, 2006
Acceptance speech before the North Carolina General
Assembly after receiving recognition for Appalachian State
University's achievement in winning the 2005 Division I–AA
National Championship

This is a creative nonfiction story based on events in the life of Jerry Moore. Every effort was made to ensure the accuracy in the presentation of events leading to Appalachian State's three national championships. Some fictional scenes, dialogue, and situations were included, with the knowledge of Coach Moore, to provide flow and continuity to this inspiring story. I hope you enjoy reading it as much as I enjoyed writing it.

Dick Brown

This book was written with the knowledge of and great assistance from Coach Jerry Moore. *King of the Mountain* is dedicated to Jerry Moore, a man of faith, a caring human being, and an amazing football coach. He is a role model for his players, whose parents don't worry about their sons playing football for him. That's because they know he is just as concerned about character off the field and in the classroom as he is on the playing field.

Jerry has shattered the old cliché that "nice guys finish last." He is the epitome of all the good-guy winners who believe in doing it the right way, and he will not sacrifice principle or honor for a hollow victory.

And a big thanks to my wife, Penny, who has patiently endured my neglect and procrastination of the many household tasks for the last three years.

CONTENTS

PREFACE

Bonham is a small Texas town on the northern edge of the Blackland Prairie not more than twelve miles south of the Red River that separates Texas from Oklahoma. The farming community located between U.S. 82 and State Highway 69 is proud of its heritage. Bonham, like many Texas towns, can trace its history back to the Battle of the Alamo. The city was named after James Butler Bonham, a defender at the Alamo who slipped out of the compound twice, desperately seeking help for Sam Houston's outnumbered volunteer army. Both times he returned empty-handed and ultimately gave his life in the struggle for Texas independence.

The legacy doesn't stop there. Other notable Americans came from Bonham, whose conservative rock-solid religious community molded their lives for greatness.

Sam Rayburn, dubbed "Mr. Sam" by all who knew him, is unquestionably the most famous native of Bonham. He served 48 years in the U.S. Congress under eight presidents and as speaker of the house for 17 terms. Like James Butler Bonham, who died at the Alamo fighting for Texas independence, Sam Rayburn died in office in 1961 fighting for a better America.

Another native son who has also achieved national prominence did so, not in Texas, but in the small city of Boone, in the heart of the Appalachian Mountains of North Carolina.

Gerald Hundley Moore was born July 18, 1939, in the sultry, dog days of summer in Bonham, Texas. Jerry, as he prefers to be called, was no less persistent than Mr. Sam. In 19 seasons as head football coach at Appalachian State University, he has led the Mountaineers to not one Division I-AA national championship but three consecutive national titles.

Appalachian State was first crowned champion after what some called a history of Mountaineer miracles. Fans and media perpetuated the label because of the exciting brand of football played by the Mountaineers. The word *dynasty* had already begun to circulate among alumni and fans in the High Country after championship number three. The modest coach brushed off such claims in his folksy Texas manner: "That stuff's for the media guys and for people to talk about over a cup of coffee."

Instead, he said those so-called miracles were the result of a strong work ethic driven by his faith in God and his personal motto: "The difference between not winning a game and not losing a game is only one thing—effort."

Surrounded by the beautiful Appalachian Mountains in the sprawling Blue Ridge range, Coach Jerry Moore has instilled his passion for the game and work ethic in the Appalachian State Mountaineers, who have become legendary for their never-quit style of play. The 69-year-old coach will start his 20th season in 2008 and is still energized by the game.

For me, a retired 70-year-old journalist, the opportunity to write a great story like this doesn't come along very often. One last shot at writing the great American story that all writers aspire to was fate. I had known about Jerry Moore 25 years before I moved back to North Carolina from Texas.

I didn't get to make his acquaintance until after his Mountaineers had finished a 6-5 season in 2004. He had changed the Mountaineer offense to a no-huddle spread formation in an effort to give them an edge in the tough Southern Conference. The first year of the new offense didn't go too well. The following thee years it improved and made history by winning three consecutive championships.

In his relaxed manner, the transplanted Texan created an offense that has been copied by other Division I-AA teams because of his great success. For years Jerry quietly studied other teams all over the country that used the spread system. He took the best aspects of what he learned and adapted them to fit the talent on his team. The I-formation that had carried him for 15 years with only one losing season was abandoned. Jerry wasn't crazy like some people thought. He was just a serious student of the game coming up with new innovations when most men his age were considering retirement.

This is a tribute to a dedicated man who still exudes that never-say-die spirit that is driven by an unshakable faith and love for the game of football.

Inspired by actual events, this story portrays the life of a shy young man from a small farming community in Northeast Texas. Bonham was a close-knit environment where church and Friday night football were the two religions. Having a Sunday school teacher for a coach inspired Jerry at an early age to become a football coach, with the same principles and faith that Coach Nelson had.

His persistence overcame a shattering midlife experience. From that challenge, Coach Jerry Moore climbed from the lowest valley of defeat in the arid plains of West Texas to the top of the highest mountain of success in Boone, North Carolina. His record is one that most coaches can only dream about, and writers can try to capture on paper.

During the last three years of his greatest achievements, the NCAA decided to make a change in the name of the two top football divisions. So you won't be confused later in the book by the switch in terminology, I will try to explain it.

In their infinite wisdom, the NCAA decided to rename Division I and Division I-AA to clear up the confusion between the two divisions. There really was no confusion among coaches and fans. It was merely a disguise to keep the bowl games' big checks going to the chosen participants and to try to make the public think it was a play-off system.

Division I was changed in 2006 to Football Bowl Subdivision or FBS, and Division I-AA was changed to Football Championship Subdivision or FCS.

The acceptance of these terminology changes has been slow with many coaches in the FCS, who still refer to their division as I-AA.

Preface

Join me in retracing the steps culminating in one man's quest to be the best in his chosen profession that took 45 years to accomplish. Jerry Moore has achieved his dream that started as a sophomore receiver in little Bonham, Texas.

PROLOGUE

> Jerry: *Come on up. We got a couple inches of snow last night, but the roads will be cleared by this afternoon. Margaret will be here, too; you can get her side of the story. When you come in the front door of the field house, turn left at the first long hallway. You can't miss my office on the right at the end of the hall. Look forward to seeing you.*

The phone went silent. Coach Jerry Moore had just agreed to tell his story about the football miracles of his Appalachian State University Mountaineers. In his 17 years at "The Rock," he is the winningest coach in Southern Conference history.

The stone fortress that the Kidd Brewer Stadium sits on is chiseled out of millenniums-old rock. It was dubbed The Rock during the 1995 undefeated season and has a huge 10-ton boulder mounted on a pedestal outside the stadium. It's an imposing reminder to all who pass that they are entering the New House that Moore built. A $32 million, seven-level expansion is scheduled for completion in 2008–2009. The legend of The Rock has grown as visiting teams have found it almost impossible to win there—the stuff of legends that every writer lives for.

"Yes!"

Photograph by Dick Brown
Kidd Brewer Stadium became known as The Rock by opponents who
found it difficult to win there. This monument stands as a symbol of
that toughness as it greets everyone who enters the stadium.

My fist punched the air with the dead phone still clinched tightly
in it. I hadn't been that excited since my story about the first earth-
quake ever recorded in Hunt County, Texas, was picked by the Associated Press.

Coach Moore and I go back to his Texas Tech coaching days. Until 2004, though, it was a one-sided relationship. I knew who he was,
but he didn't know me. The relationship started in Greenville, Texas,
where my wife, Penny, and I raised our three children. Greenville was
about an hour's drive from Jerry's hometown of Bonham.

Bonham sits right in the middle of the Blackland stratum that
cuts a jagged swath from the banks of the muddy Red River separating
Texas from Oklahoma. The stratum runs through East Texas all the
way to Mexico. The black dirt's appearance of richness deceived the
settlers who came to Northeast Texas after the Civil War seeking to
rebuild their lives. Cotton flourished in its hard, cracking texture, but
little else could survive the blistering heat and craggy plains.

An avid history lover, I discovered Bonham was the home of U.S. Representative Sam Rayburn, a great American politician and spokesman. With my two sons, Derek and Barry, I spent many hours in "Mr. Sam" Rayburn's library and his home that had been turned into a museum. They were treasure troves that documented the most important years of American history during and following World War II.

At that time I had no idea a former star football player from Bonham High School had begun to rise to the top of his profession as a college coach. His journey was long, and it took some painful detours and hit a few bumps along the way, but Jerry Moore was a man of faith and believed he could be a good football coach.

Several years later, I came to know Jerry through my son's high school football coach, Pitman Kean. Jerry was head coach at Texas Tech University at that time and Coach Kean attended Moore's summer high school coaches' clinics in Lubbock. A born-again Christian, Kean admired Coach Moore and patterned his coaching style after him. Coach Kean went so far as to outfit his Greenville Lions in new uniforms that were exactly like the red-and-black suits Texas Tech wore, even though Greenville's colors were red and white (he kept the white helmets).

Coach Moore's hard-work ethic flowed through Kean and had a positive effect on the Greenville Lions football team. The two men were great role models for their players, even though neither had winning records. The year I served as president of the Greenville Lion Backers Club, Coach Kean and I became good friends. Unfortunately, I was able to know Jerry Moore only vicariously through Coach Kean.

Following Coach Moore's Texas Tech Red Raider team was painful. The Red Raiders suffered through five losing seasons while Jerry worked tirelessly to rebuild Tech's football program from the shambles he'd inherited.

A dismal 16-37-2 record sealed Coach Moore's fate. He was fired, reaffirming the reality of the coaching profession where only winners survive. It didn't matter that almost half of those losses were by a touchdown or less. The 1985 season was supposed to be his turnaround team. Four of their seven loses were by a total of six points. Impatient Texas Tech alumni and fans said it was time for a change and proved once again that old cliché: "Close only counts in horseshoes and hand grenades."

The experience at Texas Tech shattered Jerry's self-confidence so badly that he left the coaching profession. After he left Lubbock in 1985, I lost track of him.

Our children were grown and making their own way in the world by 2004. It seemed like a good time for my wife and me to move to Winston-Salem, North Carolina. After 36 years in Texas, we were ready to move back closer to family. My three brothers and sister had stayed close to our hometown of Spencer. I was the black sheep who left the flock. It was good to be back in the Old North State.

We finally settled into our new hometown and established ourselves with the medical community. It was one of the major reasons for moving after my heart attack and several other serious health issues had occurred in a matter of two years. Before I knew it, the 2005 football season was under way and reading the sports page was the first thing I did every morning. You can't imagine my surprise when I opened it up and there was a photo with a story about Appalachian State's head coach Jerry Moore, the winningest coach in the Southern Conference. It had been over 20 years since he dropped out of sight in Texas, but there he was in a headline story of the *Winston-Salem Journal*. It was hard to believe the article was about the same demoralized man who had left coaching in disgrace after being fired from Texas Tech.

But there were clouds of dissatisfaction gathering over Boone. Moore's Mountaineers had failed to make the play-offs the last two years. Even though they had a 7-4 season in 2003, they missed making the play-offs for the first time in six years. The Mountaineers' record slipped to 6-5 the following season. That was unacceptable to many Appalachian alumni and fans that Moore had spoiled during his 16 years as head coach.

It didn't seem to matter that Coach Moore had taken Appalachian State to a record of 15 winning seasons out of 16. His teams were ranked in the top 25 nationally 12 times, made the play-offs 11 times, quarterfinals five times, and semifinals twice. As a coach he posted the winningest record in Southern Conference history. Add that to being named American Football Coaches Association Coach of the Year twice in Region 2, and the first coach to win Southern Conference Coach of the Year four times. Sports fans have notoriously short memories and there was a growing feeling of *déjà vu* at the Moore house.

By the end of the 2005 season, Appalachian had won the confer-

ence championship, swept the play-offs, and beaten Northern Iowa
for their first ever Division I-AA national championship. On December 16, the whiners were silenced for good and Coach Jerry Moore
was awarded a new three-year contract extension and a hefty raise.

He achieved everything at Appalachian that had eluded him at
Texas Tech. Winning the Division I-AA national championship made
"Moore Excitement"—the marketing slogan that fizzled in Lubbock—
come to life in Boone.

Further probing into this quiet, humble football legend revealed
another dimension of his personality. From the time he was a high
school football player, his spiritual life was interwoven with his pursuit
of football perfection. Jerry's high school football coach was also his
Sunday school teacher. He taught young Moore that living a godly life
was just as important as having a winning attitude on the football field.
His faith was established early and has been a major part of his coaching philosophy ever since.

Our first interview was in late December 2005 after the Appalachian State Mountaineers had won their first Division I–AA national
championship. I arrived early at Owens Field House for the interview
and walked unnoticed down the crowded hallway towards Coach
Moore's cluttered, trophy-filled office. The heavy traffic all seemed to
be coming from and going to Jerry's secretary Denise Watson's office
halfway down the hall. Inside her office, students were busy sorting
boxes of rings alphabetically and arranging posters to be signed. Jerry
and Margaret were nowhere in sight.

Players drifted in and out to sneak a peek at their championship
rings. There was a stack of souvenir paraphernalia to be signed for
Yosef Club members. Yosef is mountain talk for "yourself" and is the
name of Appalachian's mountain-man mascot. The club is an organiza-
tion of alumni and financial boosters who support Appalachian State
athletics.

Yosef was introduced as their mascot in 1941. He can be seen
leading cheers on the sidelines with the cheerleaders and heard firing
his long black-powder rifle every time the Mountaineers score. A larger-than-life statue of Yosef is positioned at the corner of Stadium Drive
and Rivers Street. His upraised arms that greet fans coming to every
game earned him the nickname "Touchdown Yosef."

Prologue

Photograph by Dick Brown

A larger-than-life statue of Touchdown Yosef, the mountain-man
mascot of the Appalachian State Mountaineers, greets fans at the
bottom of the hill in front of Kidd Brewer Stadium.

I entered the office and worked my way past student volunteers who were checking the guest list and stuffing invitation envelopes for the awards banquet scheduled in the team's honor. It was the highlight of the season when each team member received his championship ring.

On the back wall of the office, a large window overlooked the snow-covered field. Jerry and Margaret weren't there yet so I worked my way through the crowded room towards the eerie sight beyond the frost-covered windowpane.

Long winter shadows crept across the bleachers, turning the snow to hues of purple. A cold swirling wind sent powdery snow danc- ing across the field.

Hands cupped around my eyes, I focused on the quiet scene out- side. The window fogged up as I stood with my nose nearly touching the glass. I could hear the ghostly roar of invisible fans echoing around the chiseled-out bowl where the stadium sits.

"Sorry we're late," Jerry said, breaking my muse. He pointed to- wards a conference room adjoining his office down the hall. "We were back there trying to get the awards banquet under control. Glad you could make it."

The trim 67-year-old coach, still at his college playing weight, ex- tended his hand and greeted me with a bone-crushing grip. "This is my wife, Margaret. She's in charge and keeps me in line." Jerry winked at his wife, whose petite frame reached his shoulders.

Margaret and I shook hands and exchanged hellos and glad-to- meet-you greetings. Then Jerry led us away from the cacophony of noise spilling out of Denise's office. We came to a room with stadium seating that looked like a small movie theater where the coaches and players dissected opponents' game films.

Coach Moore's humble demeanor gave no clue that his Moun- taineer football team had won their first national championship a few short weeks earlier. The Mountaineers made history as the only college football team in North Carolina to ever win a national championship.

"Will this do for the interview? We won't be disturbed in here," said Coach Moore.

"This will be fine. Just give me a minute to get set up." I placed my tiny digital recorder on the narrow tabletop between us, pulled out my old dog-eared reporter's notepad, and scribbled across the top of the page: "First interview—King of the Mountain."

"Okay, I'm all set."

"We're all yours as long as you need us," Jerry said, as he and Margaret settled into their not-too-comfortable seats. He grinned as he shook his head, "I'm not a very interesting person. What do you want to know?"

"Everything, Coach. I want to know everything about you."

"Okay." He smiled again, took a deep breath and hunched over the table towards me. "Where do you want to start?"

"Why don't we start at the beginning, in Bonham, Texas?"

BONHAM, TEXAS

Jerry: *Bonham was just a little rural farming community that didn't have much going for it except good people, church, and football. While I was growing up, farming wasn't so big anymore. People worked for the Texas and Pacific Railroad, like my dad, or Big Smith Overall Factory, where my mom worked, and the Bonham Cotton Mill. They were the most important industries when the town started to grow. If you didn't work for one of those, you raised cattle and horses or worked for one of the downtown stores: Clayton's Grocery Store, Hunt's Dry Goods Store, McKnight's Drugstore, or the bank. We had a couple of hamburger joints; that was before fast-food places like McDonald's. There were two or three gas stations, maybe. It was really a pretty simple life. Most people were poor, but we didn't know it. One of my family's biggest events was driving 90 miles to Dallas in the summer to see a minor league baseball game. We were just a hardworking, churchgoing community that loved football.*

The 90-degree temperature felt less oppressive walking home on Graham Street into a slight northerly breeze. Jerry Moore was relieved to get out of those hot, un-air-conditioned classrooms at Bonham

High School. His shoulders drooped as he sauntered towards home. The body language was caused less by the stifling heat than by a disappointing football season, his first year on the varsity. Jerry's speed, agility, and love of football earned him a starting position as a receiver on offense and linebacker on defense for the Purple Warriors as a freshman.

Already he couldn't wait for fall practice to begin; he knew they would be better his sophomore year. After all, you can't get any worse than 0-10.

He worked hard last year and aspired to reach the heights of local football hero Bill Swoboda, a New York Giants All-Pro linebacker.

The town folks of the small Northeast Texas farming community just south of the Red River were upset that the Warriors hadn't won a single game the previous 1953 season. Next to church activities, Bonham's football team was the center of their limited social life. There wasn't much else to do in a town that, at the turn of the century, had the largest cotton mill west of the Mississippi.

Photograph courtesy of Moore family

Jerry suffered through his freshman year on the Bonham Purple Warriors team that lost all ten of their games.

Cotton was the major crop for the farmers who still worked their land, and the Texas and Pacific Railroad ran several trains through town. New industries had moved into town. Big Smith Overall Company and General Cable Plant had enticed many farmers to park their tractors in favor of a steady job with wages.

Friday night games were replayed on Saturday mornings while shopping at Clayton's Grocery Store. The Texaco station crowd stood around and talked about the game while the station attendant swept out their cars and filled them up with 19-cents-a-gallon regular.

All the community businessmen were solid supporters of Bonham High School football. They gathered for coffee at McKnight's Drugstore to discuss the poor season and coaching situation.

> Jerry: *Gene Wilshire was the leader of six or seven others who were really supportive, not just of football, but all sports. I think my junior and senior years we won a championship in every sport. You can understand why they were upset our freshman year and made a coaching change.*

Friday night football allowed everyone to forget their strenuous workweek and other problems for a few hours. Week after week the team's agony of defeat was taken on by the whole town and was a cause of great concern among its many loyal fans. They weren't used to losing.

A larger-than-usual crowd of businessmen and parents attended the first school board meeting after the season was over. After the invocation and pledge of allegiance to the flag, the floor was opened to anyone who wanted to address the board. Gene Wilshire walked up to the microphone a few feet from where the seven-member board was seated behind a long table facing the audience.

He cleared his throat, threw his shoulders back, and addressed them as though he didn't know every one of them from doing business with them in his furniture store for the previous 20 years.

"Mr. Chairman and members of the board, ladies and gentlemen, I am Gene Wilshire and would like to speak on behalf of the concerned folks you see seated here tonight. We have been talking among ourselves and think something needs to be done about the football coaching situation at Bonham High School. These boys have more talent than is showing up on Friday nights. They need discipline and direction that they

Photographs courtesy of Moore family

Coach M. B. Nelson *(left)* molded Jerry into an All-State athlete
with a strong faith in God. Coach Jim Acree *(right)* gave Jerry his
first coaching job at Corsicana High School after he graduated from
Baylor University as their leading pass receiver.

aren't getting. And I know just the man that can give them that. M. B.
Nelson is what this team needs. We . . . "

Applause from the standing-room-only audience drowned out
his words. He turned and raised his arms to silence the whistles and
catcalls coming from the group.

"We feel these boys deserve the chance to be the team we know
they can be, and we ask that the board take immediate action. That's
all I have to say. Thank you."

The room again erupted in applause and whistles from approv-
ing fans as they gave Wilshire a standing ovation.

"Will everyone please take your seats," board chairman John
Mead said, motioning the audience to sit down and come to order.
"Thank you, Mr. Wilshire, the board will take your suggestion under
advisement."

The urgency of Wilshire's request to restore the Purple Warriors
to respectability wasn't lost on the school board. In the spirit of their
most favorite son, Representative Sam Rayburn, the Bonham School
Board abided by one of his favorite quotes: "You have to go along to

get along." M. B. Nelson was hired as head coach and Jim Acree was hired as his assistant.

Nelson was a no-nonsense coach. During the week he instilled hard work and discipline on the football field, and on Sunday he instilled the fear of the Lord as their Sunday school teacher.

Coach Nelson was tough and instituted a regimented practice schedule that left the young athletes exhausted at the end of practice. But he was fair, and he inspired dedication and the will to win in his players.

> Jerry: *Everybody had great respect for Coach Nelson, the community really supported him, and the three years I was there under his coaching, everyone backed him and liked him for the man he was. That's just the kind of influence he had on us kids. He was a role model for everyone, not just the students and athletes. He was the same man every day, whether on the football field, in the classroom, or church. He was just a wonderful man. We were fortunate to have him.*

Two years later

Talmage Moore worked long hard hours to provide for his family. He gave up his job as sheriff for a better-paying job on the railroad. His absence while working the night shift for Texas and Pacific Railroad and sleeping during the day didn't make him any less supportive of his family. He took advantage of every opportunity to be with them and never missed one of Jerry's games.

As a special treat during the summer, Talmage drove the family to Dallas in their old Plymouth for three or four baseball games to see the Texas League Dallas–Fort Worth Spurs. It was an all-day trip to the metropolitan city 90 miles away. But it was worth it to Jerry, who loved sharing the little time his dad had off. The long ride gave him and his dad the opportunity to talk football.

Jerry's mother, Ruth, enjoyed the break from the Big Smith Overall factory as a sewing machine operator. It was a good job, but backbreaking work. The Moores were accustomed to the hard work and sacrifice they had learned during the Great Depression. Positive role models, they established a solid foundation of hard work, honesty,

Photograph courtesy of Moore family

Jerry's family: (*front row*) Jerry, little brother "T", and little
sister Carolyn. Behind are his father Talmage Moore and
his mother Ruth Moore.

and a strong belief in God for Jerry. Coach Nelson took that foundation and molded it into a positive attitude and work ethic that would serve Jerry for the rest of his life.

> Jerry: *My dad had very little time off from work, so I spent every minute I could with him when we went on a family trip to see the Dallas–Fort Worth Spurs semipro baseball team play. We talked about football the whole trip, which took about two hours in those days on that bumpy, narrow blacktop highway.*
>
> *I told him how some days I thought Coach Nelson was going to kill us. We ran punt-return drills over and over until we got it right. Even when we thought we had it perfect, Coach would tell us, "Run it one more time." And we ran it one more time about 10 times. My dad just smiled and said how far we had come the last two years. He thought Coach Nelson had performed a miracle with us.*
>
> *I told him how I thought we were going to do better than the year before. Everybody, including me, thought we were going to win State our senior year. Sometimes things don't work out the way you want them to.*

Excitement swept through Bonham like a Blue Norther the summer of 1956, reaching a fever pitch before practice ever started. Everyone knew the Warriors were loaded with an experienced senior team and fully expected a state championship.

Two-a-days before school started were pure punishment in the hot Texas sun, but nobody complained. The Purple Warriors were caught up in the fervor and pumped with the idea of going back to the play-offs and bringing home a state championship.

The black gumbo earth of Northeast Texas was hard and unforgiving after baking in the sun with no rain in August to soften it up. Mercifully, the final practice before school opened came to an end with Coach Nelson's shrill whistle.

"All right, bring it in here on one knee," Coach Nelson yelled as the players formed a circle around him and tried to catch their breath.

"We had success last year because we worked hard. We can't let down just because we won a district championship. It's a new season with new goals. The difference between not winning a game and not losing a game is only one thing: effort. The team with more talent didn't win a game three years ago," he said. "The same team with great effort didn't lose a league game. We have to work hard and believe we can win. Hit the showers and be on time for class Monday.

"And don't forget church Sunday," Coach Nelson reminded them as they trotted off the field.

The prophetic words from Coach Nelson were permanently implanted in Jerry's mind and became the emotional force that shaped his life. He already knew he wanted to be a football coach just like Coach Nelson.

The Purple Warriors responded to Coach Nelson's demands and hard-nosed coaching as they plowed through the first nine games of Jerry's senior season undefeated. Their last game was with nearby rival Commerce Tigers, who were also undefeated. The game would decide the district championship and who would advance to the state play-offs.

The black-and-orange-clad Tigers came to Bonham determined to go home district champions, but it wasn't to be. The Purple Warriors tamed the Tigers and won their first play-off game. Next they traveled to Dekalb for quarterfinals. Once again Bonham's season ended short of the treasured state championship they had worked so hard for. But no one complained about an 11-1 season from the team who couldn't win a single game four years earlier.

> Jerry: *Those were great games. The people of Bonham really supported us. My dad came to the last three games even though he was in the hospital. He worked at the railroad and a load of crossties shifted and fell off the flat car and pinned him down. It crushed his arm and the doctor wanted to amputate it, but my mom wouldn't let him. He spent a month in the hospital, but on Friday night, they put him in an ambulance and drove him to the games. After the game he went back to the hospital. That's how supportive he was. He was a wonderful dad. I just never told him enough.*

The quarterfinal loss was a disappointment for the team and the fans who were so accustomed to winning. Everyone believed they were primed to be state champions, but Coach Nelson wasn't disappointed in them.

Photograph courtesy of Moore family

Things improved under new coaches Nelson and Acree as the team went undefeated and Jerry was selected Honorable Mention All-District as a receiver his sophomore year.

The Bonham Purple Warriors were undefeated and won their district during Jerry's junior year. They advanced to the first round of the state play-offs, and Jerry was named first team All-District.

Photograph courtesy of Moore family

"You boys have nothing to be ashamed of," he said to the players as they slowly pulled their sweaty gear off, many for the last time. "You worked hard and played the best you could. You have had three undefeated seasons and advanced in the state play-offs two years in a row. You can be proud of what you have accomplished, especially you seniors. When we started you didn't know how to win, but you had the heart and spirit to win and achieved what nobody thought possible.

"I am proud to be your coach. Now get dressed and go out and meet your parents and friends. You have made Bonham proud."

Jerry Moore's season wasn't over though. The outstanding receiver earned first team All-State recognition as an offensive end and was named to the North Texas High School All-Star team. It was a rewarding finish for the dedicated athlete as his North All-Star team shut out the South All-Stars 28-0.

After his outstanding high school career, All-State selection, and playing in the North-South All-Star game, Jerry had his pick of any college he wanted to play for.

Undefeated during Jerry's senior year, Bonham advanced to the state play-offs. They advanced to the second round before being eliminated. Jerry was selected first team on the All-State team and played the annual Texas High School North-South All-Star game. His North All-Star team shut out the South 28-0.

Photograph courtesy of Moore family

BAYLOR YEARS

Jerry: *I was looking at Texas, Oklahoma, and Baylor. I talked to Coach Nelson about it, and he advised me against going to Texas because they had just hired a new coach. Nobody had heard of Darrell Royal at that time.*

Oklahoma was really tempting. They had won three national championships and had a 47-game winning streak going until Notre Dame beat them 7-0 that year. Then there was Baylor. Waco wasn't too far from home. So, I finally decided to go to Baylor. They had beaten Tennessee in the Sugar Bowl that year and looked pretty good to me, so that's where I went.

Waco was a bustling little city full of Baptists, located on the banks of the Brazos River. The beautiful Baylor University campus spread out on the plains, separated from the city by Interstate 35.

Jerry arrived at Baylor a raw, small-school football star who liked to draw house plans. He planned to major in architecture but hadn't thought much about it before he arrived. All he was interested in was playing football.

Registration day was a little overwhelming for the former Bonham student. He stood in long lines all day to sign up for classes that fit around his football practice schedule. When his schedule sheet was finally filled out, his last stop was at the advisor's desk.

The advisor looked at his schedule, scratched his head, and said, "Son, I think we have a little problem here. You have architecture listed as your major."

"Yes, sir." Jerry said with a little swagger in his voice, "I like to draw house plans, so I thought I would get a degree in architecture."

The advisor took his glasses off, tired from a long day of freshman registration, and looked up at Jerry. "Well, you see, son, that's the problem. Baylor doesn't offer a degree in architecture."

"They don't? Well, then I guess I'll just major in business," he shot back.

"Good." The haggard advisor scribbled his signature of approval on the bottom of the schedule.

It didn't matter to Jerry what he majored in. He knew he wanted to be a football coach and that was going to be his career.

His first year of Baylor football was a big adjustment. He hadn't been on a losing team since his freshman year of high school and Baylor struggled through a 3-6-1 season.

In spite of the poor season his freshman year, Baylor turned out to be a good choice for Jerry. He befriended Baltimore Colts All-Pro receiver Raymond Berry who came down every year at the invitation of Coach John Bridges. Bridges had been Berry's position coach with the Colts before coming to Baylor.

> Jerry: *Berry was a spindly, not-very-fast end from Corpus Christi. He taught me to be ready and work harder than the rest of them. He played college ball at Southern Methodist University in Dallas. He talked about how tough it was to crack the starting lineup because he didn't play defense very well. Back then colleges used the two-platoon system. The better defensive player usually got to start; he never started a game for the Mustangs.*
>
> *Berry only caught 33 passes in his career there. Twenty-two of those catches his senior year were good enough to make him All-Southwest Conference. He was successful because he was a dedicated athlete. His teammates liked him real well and elected him co-captain. Of course, his success in the NFL is history.*
>
> *I took lots of notes while watching game films with him. I*

kept a notebook and wrote down everything he said that would
help my game. He really was a great guy. I knew he got where he
was because he worked harder and smarter. I knew that's what I
had to do. Coach Nelson, my high school coach, preached that to
us and taught us to play with a positive attitude. Raymond was
living proof of that. He helped me a lot those years.

Jerry had found a mentor and working partner who showed him
he could make it to the pros too if he worked hard. All the techniques
Raymond Berry had used to become an All-Pro receiver he shared
with Jerry at Baylor's spring practice. Every year Jerry and Raymond
watched Baltimore Colts game films for hours after being the last ones
off the practice field.

The skills he learned from Raymond Berry paid off. Jerry was
a nationally ranked receiver by his junior year and helped the Baylor
Bears win their way to the 1960 Gator Bowl as a senior.

Both Florida and Baylor had powerful offenses that were predicted by the media to run up a big score in the Gator Bowl. To the
surprise of everyone, it was a tough defensive game with a low score.
Florida dominated the first half and Baylor fought back from a 13-point
deficit to pull within one point of the Gators, 13-12, with less than a
minute left on the clock.

The Florida defense had held the Bears to 40 yards rushing. But
Baylor had outgained Florida 211 to 57 yards with their passing game.
Leading receiver and team captain Jerry Moore led the assault that
slashed Florida's secondary with short patterns, driving relentlessly
against the clock. Inside the 20 yard line, Jerry cut in front of a defender and made a fingertip catch and battled his way to the one-yard
line before being hauled down. On their next play, the Bears broke
from the huddle with what Florida expected to be another passing formation. Instead they sent Ronnie Bull crashing up the middle for a
touchdown.

Coach Bridges knew he couldn't fool the Gators twice and called
for a pass to get the two points they needed to nip Florida 14-13.

The announcer could hardly be heard above the crowd of 50,000,
all standing for the last play as TV cameras fed the raucous scene to
millions of viewers across the country.

◊
◊

"Bobby Ply, Baylor's strong-arm passer, comes in with the play." The announcer set the formation: "The Bears break from the huddle into a balanced T-formation. Touchdown makers Bull and Goodwin crouch in the halfback slots. Minter, hands on his knees, sets up at full-back. Ends are in tight. Ply takes the snap, drops back, gets blocking help from Moore who has dropped back from his end position. Ply rifles a spiral at Goodwin in the back of the end zone. He goes high. The ball is off his fingertips! He can't hold it! Incomplete! The Gators hold Baylor off 13-12. This has got to be one of the most exciting Gator Bowl games in history!"

During the game, unknown to Jerry, a man with the same build and rugged good looks of the young athlete he was watching down on the field stood unnoticed near the stadium tunnel. He always waited at the entrance to watch the team run on and off the field. He stood close enough to the rail to touch the young athlete, but didn't. A close look was all he wanted. He felt it was all he deserved.

He wore a green-and-white Baylor booster button and spoke to a friend next to him without breaking his concentration on young Moore. "You see number 86? That's Jerry Moore, from Bonham," he said. "You'll be hearing about him. He'll make some pro team a great receiver."

The players' cleats clattered and echoed off the smooth cement walls of the tunnel. The man watched them disappear into the darkness at the other end, then turned and left the stadium without another word. He knew he would watch Jerry Moore again, just like he had for the past eight seasons of Jerry's football career.

It was a disappointing end to a great college career. But, while football was Jerry's first love at Baylor, it wasn't his only love. During his first week on campus, he met Margaret Starnes, a pretty, five-foot-seven freshman from the tiny Northeast Texas town of Mineola. She was immediately smitten by the handsome football player whose pads turned his six-foot, 185-pound frame into a giant in his green-and-white uniform.

Margaret: *It was love at first sight for me, but Jerry was so shy he would hardly talk. I knew after our first date he was the one I wanted to marry, and I chased him for three years. We never dated anyone else. We saw each other as often as we could.*

We often went to the library to study together. Our social life was pretty limited, but I didn't care. As long as I was with him it didn't matter where we went. A date usually meant going for a cheeseburger and an occasional movie. My dad sent me $15 a week allowance, and Jerry was living on his scholarship and had no spending money.

Their wedding plans had to be changed. Margaret went to summer school and graduated a semester early, anticipating their marriage after Jerry graduated. His dad had congestive heart failure after a heart attack two years before and was in declining health. So they moved their wedding date up to the spring before Jerry's senior year. Sadly, Talmage Moore passed away two weeks before they married. It was a beautiful wedding at the First Baptist Church in Mineola, Margaret's hometown.

Jerry's personal life took on a new dimension with Margaret as his number one supporter cheering him on. A new bride was the finishing touch for Jerry's senior year, which proved to be an outstanding one of personal achievements. He was ranked seventh in the nation as

Photograph courtesy of Moore family

Jerry and Margaret were married on May 28, 1960, at the First Baptist Church in Mineola, Texas. *Pictured from left:* Ruth Moore, Jerry, Margaret, Mary Beth Starnes, and Donald Starnes. Jerry's father Talmage died two weeks before their wedding.

a pass receiver and captained Baylor's Gator Bowl team that finished the season ranked 11th in the nation.

He came out of Baylor a mature young man and a well-rounded athlete. In addition to his offensive skills as a receiver, he also played well on defense, making several crucial interceptions. Earlier in his career in Waco he was used at halfback and even kicked extra points. But his greatest accomplishment, according to Jerry, wasn't achieved on the football field.

Jerry: *May 28, 1960, was the best day of my life. She actually said yes and married me; I couldn't believe it! How lucky can you get?*

BEGINNING THE CLIMB

Jerry: I was married, just graduated from college, and without a job. We had no money and no place to live. I wasn't drafted by the NFL, but the Dallas Cowboys were interested in signing me as a free agent. Pro football was more wide open than college ball and I thought I could make the team. Their rookie camp was in Minnesota, so Margaret stayed in Texas with her parents during camp.

Jerry was among dozens of players that the Dallas Cowboys had signed, desperately trying to improve on their dismal first season as a 0-11-1 expansion team. Jerry's ambition for a career in the NFL was short-lived, however. He was released by the Cowboys after only a week. When he returned to Texas, Jerry and Margaret moved in with Margaret's parents, Donald and Mary Beth Starnes, in Mineola. On weekends they drove up to Bonham to visit Jerry's mother and Momma Porter, his grandmother.

Jerry: I was lying across the bed at my grandmother's, kind of wondering what I was going to do. The phone rang and I heard Momma Porter talking to someone, but couldn't understand what she was saying. She stopped talking and the next thing I knew she came into the room and sat down on the bed with me. She sat for a minute, took a deep breath, and then looked me in the eyes.

She told me my father had just called and said he was sorry I was cut by the Cowboys. I said, "My dad died two years ago!" She shook her head and sort of acted like her mouth wouldn't work. Finally, with tears in her eyes she said, "You were adopted when you were six months old."

That shocked me so much that I jumped from my bed and took off running and didn't stop until I got to the cemetery where my dad was buried. I dropped to my knees and sat there and cried and cried and cried. Everybody knew it but me. I was heartbroken, not about being adopted; I felt guilty because I didn't think I had told him I loved him often enough.

Sometimes I wondered why they ever told me. I was 21 years old when I found out I was adopted and I cried like a baby. I hold no animosity towards my biological father, and I'm not even sure if he is still alive. I had a wonderful dad. He couldn't have been a better father to me if I had been his own son. He never treated me any differently. If my biological father didn't want to talk to me, that's okay; I had a great dad. To this day I've never met or spoken to my biological father.

Jerry and Margaret's weekend started out just like all the other weekends they spent in Bonham after he was released by the Dallas Cowboys. He wanted to gather his thoughts and try to plan a future for their young lives.

In an instant, a single phone call shattered his already uncertain life and sent him to deeper depths of despair. The comfort and refuge he usually found at his grandmother's suddenly left him like he had been struck by a bolt of lightning. Even at 21, Jerry was completely unprepared for that dose of life's reality. The sudden revelation that sent him to grieve at his dad's grave puzzled him even more when he realized everyone knew about it but him.

"Why, Momma Porter, why didn't you tell me?" Jerry asked after he returned from the cemetery.

"We never told you about being adopted," Momma Porter said, "because we didn't want you to be hurt. Your dad wanted to tell you lots of times. Remember when he would take you for car rides after church? He just never could bring himself to tell you. I guess he was afraid you wouldn't love him if you knew.

"Your Aunt Mildred was closer to your biological father than anybody else. She said he followed your football games and sort of just stood in the shadows and watched you from a distance. When you played at Baylor he would always stand down by the tunnel and get as close as he could to see you when the team ran out onto the field.

"I'm sorry you had to find out like this, but I felt like I had to tell you now in case you answered the phone if he called again while you were here sometime."

The ride home to Mineola was long and as frighteningly quiet as one of those dreams when you open your mouth to scream and nothing comes out.

"You mean you never knew you were adopted?" Margaret finally broke the silence. "Weren't they afraid someone outside the family would tell you? Kids can be pretty cruel sometimes."

"I don't know. My brother and sister knew all along, and Aunt Mildred told Momma Porter he was around a lot, but nobody knew it. He kept out of sight."

"Aren't you curious? Don't you want to meet him or talk to him?"

"Not especially. I had a great dad who loved me and wanted to be with me. If he wants to talk to me, he knows where I am."

"What would you say if he called you?"

"I don't know. If he hasn't wanted to meet me in 21 years, he probably isn't going to call now," Jerry said as the car crept to a halt in front of the Starnes' house.

Before going inside Jerry turned to Margaret. "After church tomorrow, why don't we go to Dallas and catch the Dallas–Fort Worth Spurs game for old time's sake?"

"I think that's a great idea; you need a break." Margaret leaned over, slipped her arms around his neck, and gave him a gentle kiss on the cheek. "We're going to be okay," she whispered.

Sunday broke through the early morning clouds bright and warm. It was a perfect day for a baseball game to chase away the frustrations of the events since his great years at Baylor.

They crossed Lake Ray Hubbard bridge about the same time the

Dallas skyline came into view. Just watching the sailboats drift silently across the water, powered by the morning breeze, put Jerry in a relaxed mood for the first time since learning he was adopted.

Memories of when his dad brought the family to Dallas for the Spurs' games drifted into his thoughts. Those were wonderful times that he treasured. Progress had replaced the old two-lane blacktop highway to Dallas with a four-lane interstate highway. A double bridge spanned the now full lake, once a vast pasture where cattle used to graze. The new lake was dotted with trees left by the Army Corps of Engineers to provide good fishing spots for fishermen as the lake matured.

Jerry allowed himself to enjoy the game, pushing aside the pain of the revelation of being adopted. He was a pretty good baseball player in high school and still enjoyed watching the game.

It was after 10 o'clock that night when Jerry and Margaret reached home, but he was relaxed and back to his old self. They laughed and talked quietly in the kitchen over a Coke to cool off a little. The night slipped away as he told Margaret about those long hot drives in the old Plymouth without air conditioning when he was a kid.

"It was about 98 degrees, but it felt more like 108 traveling to Dallas in August. I didn't mind it so much, but my brother and sister really whined about it. Stuff from the highway would blow in the windows occasionally. Once, all a sudden, we heard a loud smack. My sister let out an ear-shattering scream like you've never heard. A big bug had come in the window and when it hit her face it raised a red welt about the size of a dime. She didn't enjoy the ballgame very much," he snickered.

The kitchen phone rang and broke the mood of their quiet conversation. Margaret jumped up to answer it before it could ring a second time and wake up her parents.

Jerry's eyes followed Margaret, wondering who that could be at two o'clock in the morning.

"Yes, this is the Starnes residence," Margaret spoke softly. "Yes he is, just a moment."

Not sure what to expect after an unexpected life-changing call came from his biological father that afternoon, Jerry took a deep breath and grasped the phone tightly from Margaret. His knuckles were white as he lifted it slowly to his ear. "This is Jerry."

The wrinkles in his forehead quickly relaxed when he broke into a full-face grin. He recognized the voice on the other end of the line.

"Yes, sir, Coach, how're you doing? Well, after college ball, it wasn't exactly like I thought it would be. There were a lot of good athletes there; I guess I wasn't what they were looking for."

Jerry shifted his weight from left foot to his right and back again. He listened intently for several minutes, then another smile, bigger than the first one, exposed his perfect white teeth.

"I have an opening for an assistant coach and I would like to have you on my staff," Jim Acree said.

"That'd be great, Coach, but my degree is in business and economics."

"Don't worry about that. Can you come down to Corsicana tomorrow to fill out the application forms and necessary paperwork? I'll need you and Margaret to move down here as soon as you can. We start two-a-days next week. And, by the way, congratulations on your marriage."

"Thank you, sir, it's the smartest thing I've ever done. See you tomorrow. Thanks, Coach, I really appreciate the opportunity," Jerry said.

"We're going to Corsicana," Jerry said when he hung up the phone. "That was Coach Acree, my assistant high school coach. He's head coach at Corsicana now and wants me to come down there and be his assistant! Can you believe it? My high school position coach wants me to be his assistant!"

"Shhhhh, you're going to wake up Mom and Dad!"

> Margaret: *Jerry was dedicated to football at Baylor, no question about that. He never let our dating interfere with his pursuit to be the best player on the field. But when he graduated with a degree in business and economics, it never entered my mind that he would go into coaching.*

Margaret wasn't smiling.

"What's the matter? Aren't you happy for me? I'm going to be a coach! That's all I've ever wanted to do since I was in high school. And now I am going to be coaching with one of the men that taught me and convinced me that I wanted to be a coach just like him."

"Yes, I'm happy for you . . . for us." Margaret tried not to sound shocked. "It's just that your degree is in business and economics; you never said you wanted to be a coach, and you accepted without even talking to me."

"It's always been in the back of my mind," Jerry interrupted. "Football's been my whole life. I've worked hard to learn the game and how to be successful at it. And he said I can get an emergency certification to teach business math. Schools always need math teachers. You will have a teaching job waiting on you, too."

"Well, I guess that settles it," Margaret said without hesitation. "If that's what you want, then let's go for it."

"I can't believe it. Yesterday we had no jobs or plans for the future. Today we both have jobs doing what we were meant to do. This is the answer to our prayers." Jerry settled back on the living room couch to let it all sink in.

> Margaret: *We didn't have a dime when we went to Corsicana, but we were happy as larks. Jerry had four winning seasons and won a Division AAA championship in his first coaching job. High school football was such a big deal in Texas, you wouldn't believe it. I guess that's when we both got hooked on coaching.*
>
> *Coach Acree's wife, Rosemary, took me under her wing and showed me the ropes and what I had to look forward to. She was wonderful. She helped me fill the long hours of being alone, and taught me how to compete with 40 or 50 young athletes for Jerry's time and attention. I didn't know what I was getting into, and she made the adjustment much easier for me. Being a coach's wife isn't easy, but it has had its rewards. I wouldn't change it for anything.*

Becoming an assistant to his high school coach fulfilled a boyhood dream that Jerry couldn't have imagined. They worked the team just like his high school days in Bonham. Corsicana had winning seasons all four years Jerry was there and won the Texas AAA division state championship in 1963. Reunited with his mentor coach, he learned how to get the best out of his players and developed a talent for winning.

While Jerry worked days and late evenings, Margaret learned how to be a coach's wife and how to balance her life by including other people in it. It was the beginning of a sometimes isolated lifestyle she had never experienced growing up. She and her family were close and always did things together. Being alone so much was the hardest adjustment she had to make.

Jerry's success at Corsicana caught the attention of Hayden Fry, Jerry's former assistant coach at Baylor. Fry helped develop Jerry's talent as a player and saw his potential as a coach.

"You'll never guess who I talked to today," Jerry said, coming into the kitchen, where Margaret was just beginning to think about what to fix for dinner.

"You're home early, so what's up?"

"You remember Coach Fry, my position coach at Baylor? Well, he's head coach at SMU now and wants me to come up to Dallas and join his staff. What do you think?"

"If it means a raise, I'll start packing right now," she said with a snicker.

Jerry: *Coach Fry and I became good friends at Baylor and had stayed in touch. I didn't know if I was ready for a college coaching job, but the opportunity was too good to pass up. I was grateful to him for giving me my first college coaching job. We still stay in touch. He called me just last week to congratulate me on the championship.*

FROM A BEAR
TO A MUSTANG

Margaret: *It was more of the same except worse. Jerry was always gone on recruiting trips, away games, and late practices. But we managed to have all three of our children while we were at SMU. I was fortunate and didn't have to work. My children kept me busy and filled a lot of hours that would have been lonely while Jerry was gone. I had learned to get along without him being there, but he was missing their childhood and the children were missing a father. Then he had that recruiting trip incident that changed his life.*

Jerry: *Yeah, that was a terrifying experience that changed my perspective on a lot of things. I grew up in a good, honest family, but we never did many things as a family because my mom and dad both worked. I went to the First Baptist Church in Bonham and Coach Nelson was my Sunday school teacher. Margaret and I always went to church at Baylor. I had never been in trouble and lived a good life doing what I was supposed to do. I didn't want to embarrass my parents or my coaches, but I wasn't a committed Christian. Then this recruiting trip happened. I thought I was going to die. That brought me closer to the Lord.*

Photograph courtesy of Moore family

Jerry and Margaret began their family while Jerry was an assistant
coach at Southern Methodist University in Dallas, Texas. Chris and
Scott are pictured in the family photograph. Daughter
Elizabeth is in the insert.

The SMU coaching staff was meeting at the field house evaluating
the recruits who had committed, and they were scheduling who would
sign the players and when. They were all getting tired. The minute hand
on the black-rimmed, white-faced clock that hung on the west wall
of the conference room crept towards nine o'clock when the phone
rang. The noisy discussion had lost its spirit and stopped abruptly as
if someone had turned off the volume of a TV. They looked at each
other and asked with their eyes, who could that be calling so late?

The father of highly recruited twin sons who had decided to
switch their commitment to SMU wanted to know if someone could
come out and sign his sons right away. The problem was that Oklahoma was coming out to sign them at eight o'clock the next morning.
If SMU could get there first, their father said they would come to Dallas and be Mustangs.

"We can't get to Artesia, New Mexico, before eight in the morning. It's over 800 miles." Coach Fry shook his head.

"Coach, I have a cousin that's a pilot, flew Caribous in Vietnam,"
Jerry said. "We can rent a plane and fly out there tonight and sign
those boys."

Jerry and his cousin Pat Porter drove to the private White Rock
airport in Dallas and rented a single-engine aircraft. By the time they

KING OF THE MOUNTAIN

took off for Artesia it was midnight.

A strong headwind greeted them as soon as they climbed to 2,000 feet. Jerry looked down to his left and right for familiar city lights. The light aircraft shuddered and the engine groaned. It strained against the buffeting winds. When he checked the lights beneath them again, they didn't appear to be moving.

> Jerry: *The plane was moving so slow it felt like we were a kite dangling in midair. That's when Pat turned to me and calmly said, "Jerry, we have a problem."*

"What's going on, Pat? We aren't making much headway," Jerry said. "Aren't those lights below from Fort Worth and Mineral Wells? They seem to be standing still."

"The headwind is so strong it's burning up our fuel faster than I expected," Pat said. "We can't make it to Artesia under these conditions. We have to turn back and find someplace to set down," Pat said.

Pat radioed Brownsville to see if they could land there. Even though it was several hundred miles, the wind would be at their back and help them reach a safe landing place. Clearance was granted, but when Pat tested the emergency switch that should have turned on the runway lights at the airport, they didn't come on. Wrestling with the vibrating yoke with his left hand to control the wind-buffeted aircraft, Pat grabbed the radio with his free hand to call Abilene in hopes of landing there.

"This is Abilene control tower. If your gauge is registering near empty, you won't have enough fuel bucking that wind to make it here, and I don't know anywhere you can set her down in the dark. The terrain is too rough and covered with rocky ravines and scrubby mesquite trees to risk any kind of blind landing.

"There are some country roads around here. Just look for a straight stretch of highway and try to set down on that. It won't be easy with this wind, but it's your only option. I notified the sheriff's department and advised them of your situation. They have your approximate location and will be looking for you. Good luck; over and out."

> Jerry: *When Pat cut the engine at 2,000 feet to save fuel and dived down to look for a landing spot, I thought right then we*

were goners and started to pray. I didn't ask for any miracles or anything like that. I just prayed for my salvation, and Margaret and our two sons' futures. We were going down fast and I thought I would be dead in just a few minutes.

Pat's combat experience kicked in and he began a series of steep throttled-down dives. He nosed the light plane down and kept a death grip on the yoke. They bounced and drifted eastward without power, descending to treetop level desperately seeking a place to land. The aircraft's landing lights penetrated only a short distance through the inky blackness of the windy March night.

Twice he pulled up at full throttle to avoid hitting tall trees that leaped out of the darkness. On the third dive the reflection of a highway sign bounced back at them. The highway road was only a few yards beneath them. Pat engaged the throttle and revved the engine. He jerked back on the yoke with all his strength and avoided smacking nose first onto the pavement. The plane leveled off and there in front of them was the reflective center line and shoulder markings of a narrow blacktop Texas farm-to-market road.

Jerry: I had closed my eyes and prayed for my family and said my goodbyes before we hit the pavement going too fast. It was a rough landing, but we were on the ground all in one piece. The ground under my feet never felt so good. I said a prayer of thanks to God for sparing our lives.

The light plane bounced hard twice before it settled down and rolled to a stop in total darkness on a deserted rural road. It was three o'clock in the morning when Pat called the control tower in Abilene again and gave the relieved operator their location. A half hour later a sheriff's deputy arrived. He flipped on his emergency lights and instructed Pat to taxi the plane behind the patrol car. It was nearly 10 miles to the Abilene airport. Only in Texas!

A mechanic checked the fuel gauge and found it to be faulty. They weren't out of fuel as it indicated. With the fuel gauge repaired and the plane refueled, the two weary night flyers lifted off back to Dallas.

At about the same time Jerry rolled into his driveway in Dallas, the twins from New Mexico were signing with Oklahoma. A quick shower, change of clothes, and Jerry was in the air again flying to Houston to sign more high school recruits.

The Mustangs made two bowl appearances during his stay from 1964 to 1972. They lost to Georgia in the Cotton Bowl and beat Oklahoma in the Bluebonnet Bowl.

Jerry: *I don't know if I would call that trip a life-changing experience, but it certainly served as a wake-up call for me. I became more involved with my family and with the Fellowship of Christian Athletes. We formed a chapter at SMU a little later after that experience.*

As I became more involved in the Fellowship of Christian Athletes, we met Nebraska coach Tom Osborne and his family at a summer FCA conference in Colorado. They had kids about the same ages as ours and our families became great friends. After about the third summer conference he asked me if I would be interested in coming up to Nebraska as an assistant coach.

Instead of driving back to Texas from Colorado after an FCA conference, we drove up to Lincoln. We liked it and decided to take his offer. That fall Tom took Coach Devaney's position as head coach when he left and I took Tom's place.

North to Nebraska—
Top of the Mountain

Jerry: *Coach Fry left SMU and took the head coaching job at North Texas State University. They were trying to upgrade their program to get into the Southwest Conference, and changed their name to the University of North Texas. I guess they thought a name change and bringing a successful Southwest Conference coach to Denton would help their case. There just wasn't enough fan base to compete in the SWC. North Texas was mostly a commuter school. Out of an enrollment of around 25,000, there probably weren't more than 5,000 on campus. I think most people knew that getting into the Southwest Conference wasn't going to happen.*

I had already accepted an offer to go to Nebraska before Coach Fry left SMU for North Texas. It was kind of a musical chairs deal that summer. Coach Devaney left Nebraska. Tom Osborne was promoted to head coach and I took his place as receivers' coach and eventually became offensive coordinator.

Margaret: *We loved Nebraska. We found Southview Baptist, a wonderful little Southern Baptist church where the people were friendly, and we were all happy there. Jerry really enjoyed his job as a receivers' coach and assisted as offensive coordinator. He and Tom were great friends and both of our families were close and active in the Fellowship of Christian Athletes. Jerry continued speaking at churches and civic organizations in Nebraska. He never forgot his close call at SMU and accepted any opportunity to share his faith with anyone who would listen. Up until 1977, our last year in Nebraska, those were the happiest days of our lives. Being so far away from family was hard, though. My parents were still in Texas and their health was declining. I worried about them a lot.*

A cold, overcast sky met Jerry as he left the field house to meet Margaret for lunch; they always had lunch together on Fridays. She usually met him at his office, but today was different. He intercepted her in the parking lot. Lunch wasn't on his mind that day. A few minutes before she arrived, Jerry had received a long distance phone call from Mineola, Texas.

"Hey," she greeted him getting out of her car. "What's up?"

"Better get back in the car for a minute," he said, as he opened the door for her. They settled in the front seat of the still-warm car. Furrows of sadness creased Jerry's forehead as he leaned close to her. Always a man of few words, Jerry said, "Margaret, I just got a call from Mineola. Wayne Collins said your dad died this morning."

Jerry was prepared. He pulled out a fresh white handkerchief and gently blotted tears that trickled slowly down Margaret's cheeks. The news wasn't unexpected. Donald Starnes had been in poor health for years with a heart condition. But no one is ever prepared to give up a loved one, especially a parent.

"He was a good Christian man. I know he is out of pain now and in a much better place with the Lord. Have they made any arrangements yet?" she asked, gaining control of her emotions.

"The funeral is on Sunday. Mickey Skinner said he will fly us down today in his private plane."

"What about the game? You have to be here for the game tomorrow."

"Don't worry," Jerry assured her. "I'm coming right back with Mickey. He will fly me back down Sunday for the funeral. He and I'll fly back to Nebraska after the service. It's all worked out. Why don't you go back to the house and pack while I go pick the kids up at school? See you back at the house as soon as I can."

The service was held at the First Baptist Church and Donald Starnes was interred in the cemetery adjacent to the church. Margaret stayed a couple of weeks to clear up the details and business matters of the estate. She also had to make arrangements for her mother. Mary Beth Starnes, who was in the early stages of Alzheimer's disease, moved to Nebraska to live with Margaret and Jerry.

Margaret: *We had a great ride at Nebraska. They went to a bowl game every year we were there; it just became a way of life. It kind of made up for all the time Jerry spent away from home on recruiting trips. We took a little Christmas tree with us to the bowl games and had Christmas in our hotel with the children. The kids didn't think so, but I thought it was kind of nice to be in warm cities like Miami and New Orleans and leave the snow and ice back in Nebraska. In fact, Jerry's decision to become head coach at North Texas came while we were at the Orange Bowl.*

Jerry was working late reviewing Nebraska's season as co-champions of the Big Eight Conference and making preparations for their expected bid to the Orange Bowl. His phone rang.

"Hello, Jerry, this is Andy Everest. How're you doing?" Before Jerry could answer, Andy continued. "I'd like to talk to you about coming down to Denton and taking over the Mean Green football program. As you know, Coach Fry has left North Texas for Iowa and he recommended you for the job. It's yours; all you have to do is say yes."

Andy Everest was assistant athletic director at SMU while Jerry was an assistant coach under Hayden Fry. He was now athletic director at the University of North Texas. Andy's knowledge of Jerry's coaching abilities and six winning seasons and bowl bids with Coach Osborne at Nebraska made him a perfect fit for the program at UNT. Coach Fry's personal recommendation was good enough for Everest. Jerry was the only coach seriously recruited for the head job at North Texas.

"Good to hear from you, Andy. I appreciate you thinking about me, but I'm happy where I am. I have a great situation here at Nebraska and honestly haven't thought much about becoming a head coach.

I've been a position coach everywhere I've coached the last 16 years and have enjoyed it. I'm just not sure I'm interested in making a move to head coach right now."

After a few more minutes of conversation the two football men caught up the five years they had been separated and Jerry ended the conversation with, "Let me think about it some more. Good to hear from you, Andy. I'll let you know."

> Jerry: *I talked to Tom [Osborne] about it and he said, "If you have any aspirations about being a head coach, it might be a good opportunity. Offers don't come along too often, and if you want to move up to a head coaching position, take the offer."*
>
> *Well, I thought about it. Margaret and I talked and prayed about it. There were some advantages to going to Denton. It was back near both of our families in Texas. Also we had Margaret's mother living with us and it would be good for her to be back closer to other family members. So we decided if Andy called again we would take it.*

Orange Bowl 1978

The Cornhuskers had finished a light practice and were meeting the press for photo ops and signing autographs. Jerry was back at the hotel taking a break with his family. The preparation was finished. All they had to do was go out the next day and beat archrival Oklahoma. The press had called the game a tossup. The team that made the fewer mistakes and took care of the ball would win the contest.

Jerry approached each game the same way: play hard, play smart, support your teammates, and keep a positive attitude. He always told his teams if they did that, then he would be just as proud of them whether they won or lost.

"I'll get it," Margaret called from the kitchen of their hotel suite that adjoined the kids' room. "It's for you." She brought the phone to Jerry, comfortably stretched out in a recliner in front of the TV, taking in the circus atmosphere of his sixth bowl game since coming to Nebraska.

"Hello, Jerry, it's Andy. Have you given any more thought to the offer? The staff, administration . . . everyone wants you here, you're a natural for our program. Everyone is confident you can pick up where Coach Fry left off in getting us into the Southwest Conference."

"I don't know about getting into the Southwest Conference, Andy, that's somebody else's job to worry about, but I . . . we talked it over and have decided to accept your offer and come to Denton."

Nebraska came back from a two-touchdown deficit to tie the game, but Oklahoma edged them out 31-24 in the last quarter. After the game, the Moore family said their goodbyes. Back in Lincoln, they packed up and headed south to Denton, Texas.

Jerry: *We had some difficulties with the schedule, but I enjoyed North Texas. They had some pretty good Division I teams lined up, trying to prove they could compete in the Southwest Conference. They weren't even close to that level of play yet and probably never would be. I came to North Texas just to work hard and do a good job. I didn't worry about getting in the Southwest Conference, never had any thoughts about staying only one or two years as a steppingstone. I was satisfied there until the head coaching position at Texas Tech opened up. That changed everything. When they contacted me about the job, I knew that was the job I really wanted.*

FALL FROM
THE MOUNTAIN

Jerry: *I wanted the Texas Tech job more than anything in the world. I thought it was the job of a lifetime. I had worked with Tom Osborne for six years and we had one of the best programs in the country. We went to a bowl game every year and I thought I could do the same thing at Texas Tech. Even though I was warned that Tech's program was in bad shape, I didn't listen. I just wanted to coach in the Southwest Conference so bad nothing else mattered. But we failed. I was a failure. There's no other way to say it.*

Margaret: *The people of Lubbock were nice and received us warmly. We built a nice new house at the East Ridge Country Club and life was good except for Jerry being gone so much. Recruiting out in Lubbock was hard; it was a long way from everywhere. It really hurt when the people turned on Jerry and said some cruel things those last two years. If they had just been patient a little longer they would have seen the results of all of Jerry's and his coaches' hard work. The way his firing was handled was so cold and heartless. I was glad when we left Lubbock. It wasn't a good time for our marriage or Jerry's career.*

"Good morning, all you good folks out there in Red Raider land. It's going to be windy and cold today. Temperatures will be mostly in the mid-20s with a high of 32 degrees. The current wind-chill factor is a chilly 12 degrees, so bundle up before going out. Be on the look-out for an overturned 18-wheeler at the intersection of Loop 289 and Brownfield Highway. Traffic is being diverted onto . . . "

The voice of Texas Tech Red Raiders football station KKAM's early morning newscaster soon faded into the white noise of wind against the windows of Coach Jerry Moore's old Ford. He didn't feel the cold. He didn't even have his heater on as he drove along Buddy Holly Avenue. Eyes locked straight ahead, he was so fixated on coaching and oblivious to what was going on around him he had no idea he was in trouble. That was his daily routine as he made his way toward the university campus at the break of dawn.

He turned east on Broadway and caught the first glimpse of a bright burnt-orange fireball creeping above the horizon. It seemed to rise more slowly than usual this Monday morning. Or maybe his mind was just moving in slow motion. Shadows crept toward a western horizon still covered in darkness that reached to the end of the earth. From where he sat, a strong argument could be made that the earth really was flat.

A relatively young city, Lubbock sits on the high plains of West Texas atop a cap rock. Transformed from a vast lake bottom, the cap rock evolved over millions of years into a flat plain etched by the sand-blasting force of a wind that never stops blowing.

Plentiful underground water turned the arid, wind-swept plain into a desert oasis. The region has flourished since 1891 when the county government was formed and Lubbock was designated as the county seat. Cotton and the railroad put the frontier town on the map. Texas Tech University became the educational center of West Texas while Red Raider football, with their masked rider on a black stallion mascot, put them on the Southwest Conference map.

Tires screeched as troubled fifth-year head coach Jerry Moore pulled into his reserved parking space. The field house, bathed in the bright orange glow of a typical November morning, greeted him. It was 5:48 A.M. He was late for the first time in almost five years. Jerry was usually in his office by 5:00 A.M., but he was still the first person in the building. He flipped on the lights and started a pot of coffee without breaking stride.

His red-and-black all-weather Texas Tech Red Raiders parka matched his red-and-black warmup suit. He grabbed a coat hanger from the corner coatrack. When he removed the heavy coat he could have easily been mistaken for one of the team members. Daily five-mile runs and power-lifting workouts with the team gave his six-foot athletic body a much younger look than his 45 years. To demand the maximum effort from his players he felt he had to set the example—a lasting principle he had learned from his high school coach, M. B. Nelson.

Saturday's game with the Houston Cougars occupied his thoughts, blocking out the cold wind buffeting against his office windowpane. Dust drifted aimlessly, suspended in the early morning sun rays. He didn't notice.

Houston had only two wins on the season and would play their best game trying to avoid its first winless home schedule in school history. Their offense was struggling, but consistent 100-yard running backs Sloan Hood and Raymond Tate had Jerry worried.

He felt confident about his offense and emerging quarterback Billy Joe Tolliver, who had set a Southwest Conference passing record of 423 yards against Texas Christian two weeks earlier. Tech's defense had been porous, giving up too many yards and points all season. When the rest of his coaching staff arrived they had to find a way to stop Hood and Tate, he thought to himself as he gazed at a videocassette of Houston's game against SMU.

The aroma of fresh-brewed coffee filled the conference room, chasing away the new-fabric smell of sweatshirts and other promotional red-and-black attire that lined the wall in boxes. He sat down at the long table littered with yellow notepads and game tapes and started to work on Saturday's game plan. Coach Moore had been viewing Houston game films for over an hour when his phone rang.

"Good morning, Coach. Look, can you come by my office for a cup of coffee?"

T. Jones, that's what everybody called him, tried to sound natural and in command of his first season as athletic director at Texas Tech.

"Sure, I'll be right there."

The click from the other end of the line abruptly ended the conversation. Jerry put the phone down without giving it much thought; he was still running possible strategies for Saturday's game through his head. He started for the hallway.

"Good morning, Patty," he said, holding the door for his secretary, who was carrying her lunch bag and a paperback novel she read during lunch. "I'm on my way over to T. Jones's office; shouldn't be too long."

It was a short walk he had made many times to the athletic director's office, but this time would be different with his new boss.

At the end of the long hallway, less than 100 feet from Coach Moore's office, T. Jones's secretary, Mary Ellen, said in a soft West Texas voice, "Coach Moore's here, Mr. Jones."

T. Jones punched the button on his phone to hold all his calls and leaned back in his chair.

"Have a seat, Coach. Coffee?" Before Jerry could answer, Jones called out to Mary Ellen, "Bring us a couple of coffees, please."

"How do you take it?"

"Black."

Mary Ellen entered the office with a small tray trailing steam rising from the two cups. Moore wrapped both hands around the steaming cup and blew softly before taking his first sip.

Without another word, T. Jones said, "Coach, we're going to have to make a change. I have scheduled a two o'clock press conference this afternoon to make the announcement."

Coach Moore's head snapped up as if he had been hit in the back by a charging linebacker. He gripped his still-steaming cup until his knuckles were drained of all their color. Being a strong Christian, Moore wasn't quick to anger, but he was obviously surprised and upset.

He glared at T. Jones with disbelief and set his coffee cup on the desk. Jerry calmly stood up. "We have a tough game in Houston Saturday; can't you wait until next week or at least until after the game to announce it? This doesn't just affect me. My coaches need some time to tell their families. I'd hate for their kids to find out their daddies got fired from other kids at school. And you're asking these young men to play their final game of the season knowing the coaching staff has been fired?"

T. Jones paused, cleared his throat. "Okay, you have until tomorrow. I'll call the press conference for eight o'clock in the morning. Sorry, Coach, I'm under a lot of pressure. You've only won 16 games in five seasons and the alumni are really upset. It's in everyone's best interest. Don't take it personally; it's just part of the business."

The conversation was over. T. Jones stood up and walked Coach Moore to the door.

On the way back to his office, Moore thought back to 1981 when he first arrived in Lubbock to meet with his new team. He had been warned that the program was in bad shape. He was the third head coach in five years. Recruiting was in a shambles, but it was the job he wanted. He wanted more than anything else to be a head coach in the Southwest Conference.

The program's condition was even worse than the warnings he had been given. There were only 40 scholarship players at his first meeting with the team, not even enough to play the annual Red and Black game that ended spring practice. In its place, Jerry instituted a varsity versus alumni game. The event was successful for a couple of years until he recruited enough players to fill out the 85 scholarships allowed by the NCAA.

The varsity versus alumni game was popular and brought a lot of spectators to the event. His walk-on program grew to the point where 200 hopeful nonscholarship athletes showed up for tryouts. Lubbock received Coach Moore and his friendly personality with open arms. It was everything he had ever imagined being a coach in the Southwest Conference would be. Their life was good, but his football team wasn't winning.

The early honeymoon was much too short and after five losing seasons, it was over. Coach Moore felt a heavy burden of responsibility for the team's losing record. But deep inside he knew they were on the verge of breaking out as winners. He had three good recruiting years and next season he felt in his bones they would be a better team and silence the boos that had become more boisterous at Jones Stadium. But none of that mattered now. He was out and his staff would probably have to go, too.

Except for a quick call to Margaret that something was up, Moore kept his firing a secret. He went through his normal weekly pregame routine: studied Houston game tapes, met with his coaches before practice, and barked instructions and encouragement to his players during practice as if nothing had happened.

After practice, he addressed his players. "We had a good practice today. I saw a lot of hustle out there. We're coming together as a team.

It's been a frustrating season, but you worked hard and have learned to depend on each other and get it done right. We have a tough game ahead of us Saturday, but if we play up to our potential we can beat those guys."

Moore paused for a moment, his eyes squinted and furrows formed like trenches across his forehead. "When I was a freshman in high school, we didn't win a game. But we had more talent on that team than we did my last three years when we didn't lose to anybody during the regular season." Another pause for emphasis.

"Coach Nelson came in my sophomore year and taught us how to win with discipline and hard work. He gave us the will to win. The difference between not winning a game and not losing a game is only one thing: effort." He paced in front of the team, who listened intently while they rested on one knee.

"If you don't learn anything else, remember this: the team with more talent didn't win a game. The team with great effort didn't lose a game. That's it, make sure you're taking care of your studies. See you tomorrow."

The players jogged off the field to hit the showers. They were tired and sore, not only from a strenuous practice but from the lumps from 10 physically punishing games. Moore gathered his coaches in the locker room and dropped the bomb he had kept secret all day.

"I had a meeting with T. Jones this morning. I've been fired. It won't be announced until eight o'clock tomorrow morning so you can talk to your families and prepare them for the news. I'm sorry you have to go through this. I take full responsibility and will give you a recommendation and help you any way I can."

"I'm sorry, Coach." Linebacker coach Spike Dykes found his voice after a stunned silence. "We worked so hard, if they would just give us a little more time. We're almost there . . . " Without finishing, he walked up and wrapped Moore in a bear hug. "You deserve better than this," he said and walked away shaking his head in disbelief not so much about the firing but the insensitivity of announcing it just days before their last game. Being fired for not winning games is a hazard every coach accepts when he takes the job.

Quarterback coach Rodney Allison came next, and then one by one, each coach stepped forward to express his regret with a firm handshake or pats on the back.

His two sons would be okay, Jerry thought, driving home that night. Scott planned on becoming a veterinarian, and wasn't involved in the football environment. He spent his spare time working on a ranch taking care of a small herd of horses when he wasn't in school.

It would be tougher on Chris, putting him in an awkward situation as a running back on the freshman squad. But his daughter, Elizabeth, was in her senior year of high school and would be devastated if she had to leave her friends before graduation.

It was after nine o'clock when he pulled into the driveway of the beautiful ranch-style home facing the fairway of the East Ridge Country Club. Lubbock had rolled out the red carpet for him. The Red Raiders were in a slump and he was the man who was going to bring them out of it. It all seemed so long ago.

The legendary Southwest Conference of Doak Walker and Bobby Lane was one of the premier football conferences in the country. The honeymoon between fans, alumni, and any Texas football coach lasted only as long as he was winning.

The alumni had been patient for four seasons. But the undertone had gotten louder and even the supportive Lubbock *Avalanche-Journal* had deserted him. This was supposed to be Moore's breakout season and the *Avalanche-Journal* had given him the benefit of the doubt in their close losses. But there was little doubt that things hadn't improved as quickly as he had hoped after each season.

Self-doubt had crept in. Maybe he wasn't ready for the big league status of the Southwest Conference. Did he jump too quickly from North Texas State? Maybe he had it too easy working under such great coaches as Hayden Fry at SMU and Tom Osborne at Nebraska.

No, he thought to himself. He had learned how to be a winner from them and he was building a winner at Texas Tech his way, through hard work and relentless recruiting for the best players to make Tech a winning program.

Recruiting was a tough job out in West Texas. Convincing high school athletes to come out to the cap rock plains of Lubbock was a tough sell. Even more so after the Red Raiders had slipped to such a low level under a series of different coaches. He knew he was doing it right. He was at ease with his work ethic, and his faith in God was unbending. He knew this team was going to be a winner, but he wasn't going to be around to enjoy it.

Five years of highs and lows swam through his head like a school of fish darting here and there trying to escape a great white shark. He sat for a few moments longer with his head resting on his arms draped over the steering wheel. It was almost 10 o'clock. He went in to face Margaret, his wife of 25 years, and his three children who hadn't asked for this part of coaching life.

Football practice was never this tough, he thought to himself as he opened the car door. Football was his whole life. He wasn't accustomed to failure, and worst of all, he had never been fired in 24 years of coaching.

Margaret looked up from her notebook of lesson plans. "Jerry, are you okay?"

Jerry sat down next to her on the couch and spoke in a defeated voice that was unfamiliar to her. "When I called you at school and said something was up, T. Jones fired me this morning."

"Why? And why now, before your last game?"

"I don't know. I asked him to wait until after the game, but he wouldn't. He wanted to announce it to the press today. He finally agreed to wait at least until tomorrow so the coaches can tell their families. Margaret, I feel like such a failure," he said in a stronger voice after breaking the news. "I failed the kids on the team, my coaches, and most of all, you and the kids. I don't know anything but football; coaching's the only thing I've ever wanted to do."

"Don't you worry, there're a lot of teams that would be lucky to have you. We'll be okay. We'll get through this."

The next day after practice, Coach Moore gathered the team as he was accustomed to doing. But instead of his usual motivational speech, he said, "I know by now you've been hearing a lot of rumors. I've always been honest with you and I want you to hear it from me. I've been fired. Houston will be my last game with you."

Senior co-captain Sid Chambers spoke up above the murmur coming from the team members. "How can they do that, Coach? Everybody knows we're better than four and six."

"That doesn't change anything about Saturday's game. We're all honorable men here and we've worked too hard to not give our best effort. If I have given you anything while I've been here, I hope it is the will to win, no matter what the situation. Being a good football player is about more than what you do on the field. It's the kind of man you are and how you conduct yourself off the field as well."

The rumble of confused and disappointed athletes grew louder.

"Okay, listen up. We're going to keep our focus this week and go down to Houston to win a football game. Get some rest and come prepared to work hard tomorrow."

The noisy conversation of 97 players filled the dining hall, then hushed when Coach Moore walked into the room for their final Thursday night meal together. It was his tradition to always eat with the team every Thursday evening in their dining hall.

Tonight would be special. He had watched the seniors grow from his first class of green freshmen into mature football players and young men. There were underclassmen like sophomore Billy Joe Tolliver who he knew would have a great future in professional football.

Everyone ate dinner and tried to act as if nothing had happened. One hundred fifty steaks, 100 pounds of potatoes and vegetables were consumed in less than an hour by the hungry athletes.

He pushed his chair back as he stood up to leave, and spoke to the team. "I just want to say I am proud of how you stuck together this week and concentrated on Houston. Our plane leaves at three o'clock tomorrow. Make sure you're here on time; the bus won't wait. Get a good night's sleep and remember you're a team. You've worked hard and you depend on each other out on the playing field. See you tomorrow."

At home with his feet propped up on his favorite hassock, Jerry finally let the strain of a trying week drain from his body. The phone rang.

"It's for you," Margaret said. "It's Jess."

"What could Jess want? I just talked to him at dinner."

Assistant athletic director Jess Styles and Coach Moore were good friends. He often attended team dinners and liked to interact with the coaches and players. This final dinner was different than any before it. Emotions ran high and simmered just below the calm surface shown by the players.

"Coach, we've got a problem. You better get back up here!" Styles said. "They aren't going to play; they are going to boycott the game with Houston! You need to get here quick."

"I'll be right there." Jerry hung up the phone and turned to Margaret, still standing next to him.

"What's the matter, Jerry, is something wrong?"

"Jess said the players aren't going to play Saturday. I have to go and get this thing under control." He pulled on his coat as he rushed out to quell a team revolt.

There was a rumble like a spring thunderstorm rolling out into the hallway from the dining hall when Coach Moore entered.

"Okay, what's this all about?" Moore asked calmly. He was an easygoing man who didn't have to swear or yell to get the players' attention or respect. It was against his nature and religion to do so. His assistants did the shouting during practice drills and on the sidelines on game day.

Joe Chase spoke up. "Coach, the team feels like we've been betrayed, and we don't want to play. We aren't going to Houston tomorrow."

"I understand your feelings, but things are bad enough. Don't do something like this; it'll just cause a big stink and make things worse. We have a commitment to play Houston on Saturday and as honorable men we have to uphold that commitment. Principles you learn in the game of football will guide you the rest of your life. It's all about making choices and doing the right thing. I want to see everyone on that bus tomorrow."

Before leaving the room, he cornered the four team co-captains: Sid Chambers, Tim Crawford, Joe Chase, and Mike Kinsey.

"You men are the team leaders; they look up to you and respect you. I'm depending on you to make sure everybody shows up on time to go to Houston. I know you won't let me down. See you tomorrow."

Players' duffel bags were being loaded in the luggage compartment of the charter bus while assistant coaches checked to make sure all the players were accounted for. The equipment managers loaded the heavy trunks of uniforms and gear necessary to support the traveling squad.

"Hi, Margaret," Coach Dykes said. "Good to see you. The team isn't used to you traveling with us; they'll be glad to have you on board."

The ride to Lubbock International Airport was uncharacteristically quiet. When the buses unloaded on the departure dock it looked like an invasion and drew stares from small children who marveled at the size of the big linemen. A few scattered fans waved and wished them good luck as they filed through the gate to the waiting aircraft. They entered the empty charter jet single file, taking seats as the line made its way to the rear of the cabin.

Jerry took Margaret's hand and led her to a pair of empty seats in the midsection of the aircraft. "Normally I sit up front with the other coaches, but today I think we should sit among the players."

The gesture was welcomed by the players. They relaxed and talked among themselves and with the coach and his wife for the hour-and-a-half flight to Houston.

When the plane touched down at Hobby Airport, the reality of the last week began to bubble back to the surface. It was their last game playing for a coach who had poured his heart into molding them into winners on and off the field.

There was little chatter in the dressing room as the players pulled on their pads.

"Let's win this one for Coach Moore!" Billy Joe Tolliver high-fived Tyrone Thurman and pumped up the team's emotions as he led them cheering and whistling through the tunnel onto the Houston Astrodome turf.

The pop of leather against leather on the opening kickoff cleared the air. Like the pistol shot to begin a race, it released the raw anger and frustration that had festered all week.

Defensive coordinator Jim Bates shouted and pumped his fist into the air. "All right, good hustle, Johnson!" Johnson had recovered Sloan Hood's fumble on Houston's 34-yard line. The turnover resulted in a Tech field goal for an early 3-0 first-quarter lead.

Two long Houston drives led by quarterback Greg Landry quickly put the Cougars up by 11 points. A Tech field-goal attempt to narrow the gap hooked wide to the left as the first half ended.

The second half began with Houston in control 14-3 and the Cougars kept the pressure on with aggressive defensive play and added a field goal in the third quarter. A missed field-goal attempt by Tech ended the third quarter with the Red Raiders trailing 17-3.

The dominating Houston defense had pressured Tolliver all afternoon into making hurried throws. Sacked twice when he couldn't find open receivers in Houston's tight coverage, the Southwest Conference's leading passer had been frustrated all afternoon.

The scoreboard clock showed only five minutes left in the game.

"Come on, let's show 'em who we are," co-captain Joe Chase shouted to the defense as he moved up and down the line, slapping them on their backs. "We gotta give the ball back to the offense, we gotta do this for Coach."

The Red Raider defense held the Cougars to only four yards on three straight running plays and forced them to punt. Tolliver took charge and did the rest. He drove the Red Raiders down the field with a combination of short passes, spread among four receivers, and quick bursts up the middle of a suddenly confused Houston defense.

On third down from the 18-yard line, Tolliver found running back Ervin Farris open in the flat. He caught the pass in stride, shook off his defender, and scampered 10 yards into the end zone.

Moore shouted at his defense as they trotted onto the field. "Okay, let's get it back, we still have time."

Houston, still confident that their running game could run out the clock, alternated Tate and Hood, who pounded the Red Raider line. Again Tech's defense held Houston to only six yards on their 33-yard line and forced the Cougars to punt with less than two minutes to play.

"It's a high spiral kick that's going to stay in bounds and force a return by Texas Tech," the announcer's voice droned over the Houston airwaves.

Every player on Tech's bench crowded the sidelines for the special-team punt return and grimaced when five-foot-five "Tiny" Tyrone Thurman fielded the ball on his own 11-yard line. The scowls turned to cheers as Thurman juked his way past the first Houston defenders.

"He's up to the 20. Thurman cuts across the middle and finds an opening." The announcer's voice rose as he described a sure highlight-of-the-week play as it unfolded down on the field. "Thurman's at the 50 . . . the 40 . . . he may go all the way! Only one man between him and the goal line. It's a footrace and . . . Thurman is brought down from behind at Houston's 11-yard line! Safety Robert Jones came all the way across the field to make the touchdown-saving tackle on Thurman!"

Two plays later, fullback James McGowen's three-yard plunge into the end zone put the Red Raiders within one point of the Cougars. The clock had run down to 56 seconds.

"Time out! Time out!" Coach Moore yelled to the sideline referee only a few feet away. Tolliver trotted over to the sideline. The coaching staff gathered around their quarterback. "We're going for two." Coach Moore made close eye-to-eye contact and said, "Play option look . . . we practice this every week. Flood the end zone and make it work. Let's go!"

The announcer leaned forward to get a better look at the two teams as they lined up. "Tolliver brings the Red Raiders up to the line of scrimmage. He checks the Cougar defensive alignment and moves under center. He barks the signal for their last shot at giving Coach Jerry Moore a farewell victory.

"Tolliver pulls out, fakes a handoff in the middle. He rolls to his right, checking his receivers. He's got a man open in the end zone! Tolliver fires a bullet towards Farris! It's tipped! The pass was tipped! Linebacker McGuire knocked it away at the last second; Houston wins! The Cougars laid it all on the line today and dodged a losing home season!"

Giddy fans streamed onto the Astrodome field, hugging and back-slapping the jubilant Houston players.

Tech players' heads drooped in disbelief. Big brawny men sagged like all the air had been sucked out of them as they trudged off the field.

Coaches and players tearfully shook hands and hugged each other in a solemn dressing room.

Reporters, who had been feasting on Tuesday's announcement of Coach Moore's firing, swarmed the pressroom. Deflecting questions about being fired, Jerry instead talked about his team.

"It was a tough loss," Coach Moore said, wiping away tears, "but these guys gave their best effort every time the ball was snapped. I've learned enough in five years at Tech to get me through whatever is ahead. If I can compete like these guys did, then my life is going to be in good shape."

Jerry: *They were a great bunch of players. I still hear from some of them. Tolliver had a great pro career and called to congratulate me on the championship. I was proud to see them succeed and would love to have been there with them, but that's how it works in this business. I have no regrets, I love it here at Appalachian. Things couldn't have worked out any better.*

SOUL SEARCHING

Margaret: *I was angry and bitter and knew I had not
been living the kind of life my Baptist family had raised me to
live while growing up in Mineola. I had my adolescence rebel-
lion in my 40s. I sort of got even by having my friends over for
parties while Jerry was out on the road. I went places without
him, which I had never done. I lived a more social life than ever
before. I was never unfaithful, but my heart and mind weren't in
the right place during those years in Lubbock. It wasn't a good
time in our marriage.*

*Having to listen to all the ugly things that were being said
about Jerry hurt. They didn't appreciate how hard he had worked
and how he neglected his family to build a winning team there.
Many nights he slept in his office and it seemed like he spent the
rest of his time on the road recruiting. It was his dream job and
he wanted to be as successful as he was at Nebraska. Jerry was a
good recruiter and he did what it took to get the players he needed. It just meant he was gone a lot, and we missed him terribly.*

*Our faith, and the inscription we had engraved on the in-
side of our wedding rings when we were first married, helped us
through those tough times. Jerry's aunt wore a bracelet that had*

it inscribed on a charm, and we both loved it. It said: "Love, it means more tomorrow than it meant today. When I see you today, I love you more than I did yesterday. I love you more and more each day." It's just as true today as it was then.

Everything Jerry had worked for in his last 24 years of coaching was taken away. He had moved up from receivers' coach to offensive coordinator at one of the best college programs in the country at Nebraska. He carefully studied Coach Osborne's methods and added his own techniques to build a powerful, sustaining program.

Osborne gave him a free hand with the offensive system, and Jerry recruited the talented athletes to make it successful. Nebraska's offense was envied by other Division I coaches, especially by his good friend Danny Ford. Ford invited Jerry to Clemson to teach his Tigers Nebraska's offense. Those were the good times—six straight winning seasons and six major bowl games while he coached at Nebraska were a distant memory now.

His office was cleared out except for a few boxes loaded with personal items. There were letters from grateful parents thanking him for helping their sons become better young men and students, not just better football players.

There were no championship trophies or plaques of gratitude for rebuilding the badly broken program that had greeted him when he arrived. None of that. Just the echo of T. Jones' voice,— "Coach, we're going to have to make a change"—and the thoughts of what might have been if he had been given a little more time.

> Jerry: *We had the talent. I prayed about my mission as a coach and mentor, and my conscience was clear. I had done everything I could for the success of the Texas Tech program.*
>
> *I wasn't ready for a Division I head coaching job. I thought I was, but I wasn't. We recruited well. It was just a matter of time. The players we recruited went to bowl games two of the next three years and sent eight players to the NFL. But that's just the way it is in the coaching business.*

Alumni and rabid fans didn't put much stock in what could have been. They lived for the rush of victories every Saturday, for the delirium of conference championships, and for cheering their beloved Red Raiders on in the Cotton Bowl in December.

Jerry gently placed the final items from his desk, pictures of his wife and kids, into a box. It was time. He picked up the box and took one last slow look around his office. It was as quiet as a tomb for the first time in five years. Emotions of failure, frustration, and relief all mixed up together forced a deep sigh as he walked out of the field house for the last time. He had no regrets.

Driving out Buddy Holly Avenue toward home before dark felt strange to the dedicated coach who seldom left the field house before 10 o'clock. He bade farewell to the rock & roll legend's larger-than-life statue and turned west toward an Ansel Adams picture-perfect sunset and home.

Five years of memories, good and bad, were neatly stacked against the garage wall. Inside, the rest of the Moore family gathered in the den to discuss what was going to happen next. They had moved before with Jerry's job changes, but being fired was a new and unpleasant experience.

"Don't worry," Jerry told his children. "Your mother and I talked about it and we aren't going anywhere."

Elizabeth's face reflected the uncertainty the three nearly grown children all felt but would not say out loud.

"We'll stay right here in Lubbock until we get things worked out. I'm not going to do anything to disrupt your lives. Elizabeth, we want you to finish high school here in Lubbock with your friends. If I get a coaching job somewhere else, your mother will stay here with you. And you boys can either stay at Tech or transfer to another school. They bought out the last two years of my contract; we're going to be okay."

Air returned to the tension-filled den. It had felt like a vacuum before those words of assurance came from Jerry. The moves had become more difficult as the children matured and developed close friendships, especially for their middle son, Scott. He didn't want to leave Lincoln or Denton and was miserable for the first year in Lubbock.

Chris and Scott had grown to like Lubbock and accepted the change easier than Elizabeth.

Chris broke the ice. "Dad, I'll finish out the year here and see how it goes."

Jerry knew it would be uncomfortable for Chris. Being the former coach's son still on the team would be a strain emotionally for him and might be awkward for new coach David McWilliams. Tech had hired McWilliams away from the University of Texas with visions of national championships in their eyes.

"I understand," Jerry said. "Whatever you want to do is fine with me."

"What about you, Scott?" Margaret asked.

"I like it where I am, working on the ranch, helping with the animals and all. It's good experience for me and fits my plans to go into veterinary medicine."

"Sounds good," Jerry said. "Now there is something I need to talk to you about, but I wanted to hear your thoughts first.

"Danny Ford called me Tuesday morning as soon as he heard I was fired. You know what good friends we became when I was an assistant at Nebraska. He's head coach at Clemson now and doing a really great job." After a short hesitation Jerry said, "He offered me a coaching position. Your mom and I are going up to check it out."

Jerry had a lot of respect for Ford. At age 30, Ford became the youngest head coach in Division I football. His first game as head coach, after the resignation of Charley Pell, was against Ohio State in the 1978 Gator Bowl. Clemson upset the Buckeyes 17-15 and the hot-tempered Woody Hayes drew a penalty for punching a Clemson player in front of the Ohio State bench. It was Hayes' last game as a coach. Ford went on to take Clemson to an undefeated season and their first national championship in 1981, beating Jerry's former team, Nebraska, 22-15 in the Orange Bowl.

Jerry: *I've always made a practice of studying other teams to learn anything I could to help our team. Danny Ford and I became good friends and we exchanged ideas. When I was offensive coordinator at Nebraska, he invited me down to Clemson to teach our offense to his coaches and team. Later, I took my coaching staffs from North Texas and Texas Tech to Clemson to observe how Ford's successful Division I program operated and bring back what we could use in our system. We watched everything they did in meetings and on the field.*

The inner circle of college coaches was a close-knit group, almost like a fraternity. They helped each other out when times were tough and Ford wanted to help his good friend because he knew he was a good coach with a creative football mind. Pat Dye, head coach at Auburn, also called Jerry to offer him a job.

The trip to Clemson, South Carolina, was a whirlwind tour of the state-of-the-art facilities in Death Valley, the affectionate name given the football stadium that sat in a naturally sunken valley on campus. Ford and his coaching staff welcomed Jerry and Margaret and made them feel right at home. The Moores liked what they saw. They even looked at housing during a short break. Jerry had long been impressed with the Clemson program and knew what a big opportunity he was being offered. Clemson was a powerhouse in the Atlantic Coast Conference, nationally ranked in the top 10 regularly with an enviable bowl record.

"What do you think?" Jerry finally broke the silence a half-hour into their long drive back to Texas. Without waiting for her answer, he said, "It's a good opportunity and a great program."

Margaret just listened; it was so seldom he talked about his work. When he came home at night they never discussed football. He left it at the field house or on the practice field with the team. Football wasn't a topic of conversation between them. She wanted his undivided attention during the precious few hours he was away from the sport.

"But it just doesn't feel right. I would be up there, a long way from you and the kids in Lubbock. I don't think it's fair to you and the kids."

By the time they reached Lubbock, Jerry had talked himself out of accepting the Clemson job. The next day he also turned down the offer from Pat Dye at Auburn University. It was a time to keep the family together and start the healing process of rebuilding his self-confidence.

The hurt from being fired ran deep, but Jerry leaned on his family and faith for strength. At age 46, he thought he was finished as a coach, the only thing he had ever wanted to do. It was time to find a career to use his degree in business and economics, to start a new life out of football that would support his family.

Two days after their return from South Carolina, a third job offer came. When Jerry answered the phone he was surprised by the voice on the other end of the line.

"Hey, Coach, it's time to hang up your jock and come to work for me and make some real money," Jerry Stiles said. "Something you should have done a long time ago. They have done you a favor, my friend. Come to work for me in Dallas and you will make more money than you'll ever make in football. You'll be outdoors, playing golf and talking to clients. You're a natural. What do you say?"

Dallas businessman, Jerry Stiles, was an entrepreneurial heavyweight with his financial fingers in several enterprises. He was part-owner of the Dallas Mavericks NBA basketball team, and his Hallmark Mortgage Company was one of the largest companies in the Southwest.

The job was one most people would have killed for. The trip to Clemson postponed Jerry's urge to stay in coaching, at least for the present time. The desire was still there, but of his self-confidence was in need of repair. Jerry needed some separation from football for a while.

Jerry: *I had a great job making a lot of money. I traveled and played a lot of golf—even came up to North Carolina on a project in Charlotte. I was based out of Dallas, but had an apartment in Atlanta working on a country-club project there. Margaret and I spent more time together while I was in Atlanta than we had since we were married. We had a beautiful lake house we built in East Texas, but we didn't live in it much. Margaret quit teaching in Mount Pleasant and came to live with me in Atlanta. Life and business were good.*

LIFE OUT OF FOOTBALL

Jerry: *I was faking it; I'd come back to Atlanta from long road trips and cry myself to sleep at night. I had a good job, but I was miserable. I wanted to get back into coaching. Finally, Margaret joined me in Atlanta. There was a lot to do there. Atlanta has some really good restaurants. It was good to be back together again; she helped me get through those bad days.*

Margaret: *Deep inside I knew he was unhappy. The facade he had put up for everyone was pretty convincing, but I knew him and saw through it. The more the pain of disappointment and failure at Tech faded, the more he wanted to get back into coaching football. I just waited for the time when he had had enough.*

Jerry had convinced himself not to take a new coaching job with the rationale of keeping the family together. He did that . . . sort of. Jerry Stiles was very persuasive and made Jerry Moore an offer he couldn't refuse.

The next week after he and Margaret returned from Clemson, Jerry was being introduced to the staff of Hallmark Mortgage Company as their newest field manager. Hallmark was one of the largest and fastest-growing real-estate development companies in Dallas.

Scouting around the South and Southwest looking for development projects and builders that needed financing kept Jerry on the road most of the time. Margaret couldn't join him until Elizabeth graduated from high school in the spring.

November and December dragged slowly. The rest of the year was an unpleasant experience for Chris. His decision to stay at Texas Tech didn't work out the way he had expected. He planned to transfer to Stephen F. Austin the next year and be a running back for the Lumberjacks.

Jerry flew out to Lubbock on weekends, which helped the family get through the rough spots in their new life. Spring finally arrived with beautiful Texas bluebonnets and Indian paintbrush wildflowers chasing away the dark brown of winter's death. Hues of bright blue and orange covered the banks along highways like thick carpet. They were everywhere, a beautiful sight for Lone Star State travelers.

By the end of summer, their house in Lubbock had sold. Elizabeth decided to stay in familiar territory with some of her friends and enrolled at Texas Tech. Chris had packed off to Nacogdoches and was settled in his football dorm and ready to start fall practice with the Lumberjacks. Scott, who wasn't involved in football, stayed at Tech and pursued his studies in pre-veterinary medicine. He also kept a close eye on his little sister, Elizabeth.

Jerry had a small apartment in Dallas and commuted to their new home on Lake Cypress Springs in East Texas. It was Margaret's dream house; they thought it would be their home for life. It was good for them to be out of Lubbock. Relieved of the stressful pressure of trying to build a winner in the powerful Southwest Conference, they could start their new life in a different world.

It was just the two of them and they spent more quality time together than they had in all the years they were in Lubbock. But things changed. Jerry was sent to Atlanta on a project there. He had an apartment and commuted home to Texas every weekend.

Jerry: *I was earning more money than I had ever made in my life. We could afford to have all three children in college, living in apartments off campus. They each had their own cars; things were going really well financially for us. I was putting up a pretty good front, I thought. But then I began to travel more and was sent to Atlanta on a big project. Margaret stayed home in that beautiful house and taught school at Mount Pleasant. I hate I didn't get to spend more time there.*

Margaret: *After Jerry was transferred to Atlanta, things got tough. He was wearing himself out commuting to Texas every weekend. And I was in the middle of the semester teaching school. Finally, I told the principal that I had to leave at the end of the semester in December. It was just too hard on Jerry and wasn't good for our marriage.*

We kept the house and I moved to Atlanta to be with Jerry. We had a ball in Atlanta. We went to movies and ate at some really great restaurants. We love Mexican food and there were some good Mexican places to eat. We played a lot of tennis. It was fun, just like being newlyweds again. We were happy with each other, but I knew he wasn't happy with his job.

New projects and company growth in the South and on the South Atlantic coast forced Jerry to temporarily take residence in Atlanta to work on a major project—building a new country club and golf course. From there he traveled up the east coast to North Carolina for a shopping-center project in Charlotte and a business-park project in the Raleigh/Durham Research Triangle.

Clemson, South Carolina, was only a short drive from Atlanta. During the fall of 1987, Jerry visited his old friend Danny Ford on home-game weekends. Ford gave him free access to his coaches and team on his visits.

The more time he spent with Ford and his Clemson Tigers, the higher his confidence level grew. He sat in on locker-room talks; he walked the sideline during games like he was one of the coaching staff. He spent the second half in the press box and observed the coaches up there calling offensive and defensive plays to the bench. Jerry was a serious student of the game and listened to everything that was said in the locker room before the game and during halftime. He picked the football brains of Ford and his coaching staff at every opportunity.

As he drove back to Atlanta from Clemson's final home game

he realized his team at Texas Tech wasn't that far away from being a winner when he compared them to Clemson. He was frustrated and proud that his replacement, David McWilliams, had posted a 7-4 record and was going to play Mississippi in the Independence Bowl.

He felt vindicated that his effort at Tech had finally paid off—they were winners. That was all the reassurance he needed. Jerry knew he belonged back in football. His nights of depression and crying himself to sleep and pretending to like his job were over. With renewed confidence, he put out word that he was ready to get back into coaching. His first call was to Ken Hatfield, head coach of the Arkansas Razorbacks.

"Hello, Ken, this is Jerry Moore. I just wanted to call and let you know that I'm back in the market for a coaching job. I'm not asking you for a job, just wanted you to know I'm back in the hunt, and if you know of any openings, I would appreciate a good word from you."

"Glad to hear that. I don't have anything open right now, but I'll sure keep my ears open for you. Welcome back; this is where you belong. You'll find the right job; you're too good a football man not to be in coaching."

Ken Hatfield's Arkansas teams were always a powerhouse in the Southwest Conference, as well as a bowl contender. Jerry and Ken had been friends since Jerry was an assistant coach at Nebraska and Nebraska played Arkansas many times during Jerry's stay in Lincoln. There was a lot of camaraderie among coaches at the Division I level as assistant coaches moved around waiting for their chance at a head-coaching job. Before their conversation ended, Hatfield offered Jerry a job. But not the job he was looking for.

After a short pause, Hatfield said, "Look, Jerry, I don't have a paid position open, but why don't you come on up here as a volunteer for a while?"

"Volunteer!" Jerry said, trying not to laugh into the phone. "Coach, I've got three kids in college, a lake house in Texas, and five cars to support."

"I understand, but think about it and let me know if you change your mind."

Jerry put his hand over the phone and looked at Margaret. "There's no way we can afford to do that. He offered me a job as a volunteer coach."

"Sure we can," Margaret said. "You aren't happy doing what you're doing. If you want back in coaching, let's go."

That was all the encouragement Jerry needed. Salary or not, he knew he wanted to go to Arkansas the minute Hatfield made the offer.

Jerry hung up the phone more excited than he had been in a long, long time. He turned to Margaret. "He's built a really great program at Arkansas. They've played in a bowl game every year he's been there with better than a 70 percent winning average. This could really be great. I know it's going to be tough and I don't know how we are going to afford it, but it's an opportunity I can't pass up. Thank you for being so understanding."

"Don't worry; I'll get a teaching job," Margaret assured him, "and we'll live like a couple of college students. We can do it. It might even be fun!"

Margaret: *The old competitive fire was back in Jerry's eyes. Whatever doubts I had about coaching for free were gone. I hadn't seen him this excited since he took the Texas Tech job. We packed a couple of suitcases and spent a restless night. Before daylight the next morning, we were headed west on I-20 for Fayetteville.*

BACK IN THE GAME

Jerry: *We came into Fayetteville, Arkansas, inconspicuously and moved into a little $200-a-month apartment. It was a flashback to our first year of marriage at Baylor. We drove up there with only a couple suitcases of clothes. It was kind of ironic. We had a beautiful house on Lake Cypress Springs. It was Margaret's dream house because she had it built just the way she wanted it. It was sitting there full of furniture with nobody living in it. Going to Arkansas was a clean break for a new beginning and getting back into coaching. I was really excited about that.*

Margaret: *I knew it was a big leap of faith, but it was the best thing we ever did. I was able to get a teaching job while Jerry worked his way into a paid staff position. We prayed about it and felt God had opened a door for us. It was up to us to make it work, and we did.*

Ken Hatfield had a lot of respect for Jerry Moore as a man and a coach. Hatfield had coached against him when Jerry was offensive coordinator at Nebraska and the Cornhuskers ran roughshod over his Razorbacks. Although the Southwest Conference coaches were competitive as opponents on Saturday, they were friends off the football field. They shared stories and even gave advice to each other on the golf course at coaches' conferences in the off-season.

They were like fraternity brothers, hurting for a friend who might be having a bad season or who had gotten fired. They were often close friends like Jerry and Coach Danny Ford at Clemson.

It was ironic that after Jerry left Nebraska and was in his first season at Texas Tech, Nebraska met undefeated Clemson for the first time in the Orange Bowl. Clemson won that game 22-15, claiming its first national championship after posting its first undefeated season in school history. Was Jerry's help in teaching Clemson Nebraska's offense the edge they needed to win? Maybe, maybe not; that's just one example of what close friends coaches can be.

Now Jerry Moore was being extended a helping hand by an old Southwest Conference adversary to get him back into the game he loved. He was willing to work for no pay just to get back into football. But his talent was quickly put to good use working with Arkansas receivers and the offense.

Hatfield knew how hard Moore worked at Texas Tech, and every day after practice he kicked his assistants out of the office and told them to go home to their families. If a coach's child had a recital on a Thursday night, Hatfield told him not to even think about it, just go. On Sunday nights, all the coaches and families had dinner together.

"Too many coaches never see their kids," Hatfield said once, admonishing his coaches to spend more time with their families. "One of these days you're gonna be without a job, and when Thanksgiving comes and everyone's talking about their family memories, you won't have anything to say."

Ken Hatfield wasn't the only one who knew the kind of man Jerry Moore was, or knew about his talent for getting the best out of his players. It was just a matter of time until that talent was uncovered, and he became a coaching legend in his own time.

Margaret approached Jerry as he entered the tiny kitchen of their apartment. "I have a great idea, let's go out and eat Mexican tonight."

"Give me a few minutes to change; I've got some great news." Jerry pulled off his red-and-white Razorback sweat suit. "Ken wants me to help out with the offense this spring. I think he may offer me a promotion to offensive coordinator!"

"That's great, Jerry!" Margaret said. "The good Lord takes care of His own. I'll look over tomorrow's lesson plan while you're getting cleaned up."

The phone rang and Margaret put down her notebook.

"Hello," she said, expecting their daughter Elizabeth's voice.

"Margaret, this is Jim Garner, how are you and Jerry doing out there in Arkansas?"

She thought that sounded a little strange, because he was at Texas Tech when they left, and Arkansas is northeast of Lubbock.

"We're doing fine, how are things in Lubbock?"

"I'm not at Texas Tech anymore. That's kinda what I need to talk to Jerry about. Is he available?"

"Just a moment. Jerry, it's Jim Garner for you." She shrugged her shoulders, looked at Jerry with wide questioning eyes and handed him the phone.

"Hello, Jim, good to hear from you."

"Same here, Coach. Look, I left Texas Tech and am now athletic director at Appalachian State University up in Boone, North Carolina. The head coaching job is open. Coach, Sparky Woods left for the head coaching job at University of South Carolina. Are you interested?"

"Well, yeah, but where is Boone? I've never heard of Appalachian State."

"They're a Division I-AA school but play in a really tough league. The mountains take a little getting used to, but I think it's a good situation for you. They have a great program in place and a long winning tradition. It's nothing like the situation when you arrived at Tech. Talk it over with Margaret and get back to me. The job is yours if you want it."

"Okay, Jim. Thanks for thinking of me, I appreciate it."

Jerry hung up the phone and turned to Margaret, laughing and shaking his head. "Margaret, get the road atlas; we have to find out where Boone, North Carolina, is."

Jerry: *It was really good to hear from Jim. We were good friends at Tech. He enjoyed being around the players and usually ate with us on Thursdays. His offer to come here [to Boone] came out of the blue. We had settled in at Arkansas, and I enjoyed working with Ken Hatfield. He was a really neat guy. But I felt like I was ready to take another shot at a head coaching job. Appalachian sounded like a good fit for us. I wasn't too sure about living in the mountains after living so much of my life in the flatlands of Texas. We wanted to check it out before making a decision. I didn't want another deal like Tech.*

SECOND CHANCE

Jerry: *I flew up there and called Margaret back and told her she wouldn't believe this place. It's like a picture postcard. I spent the afternoon in meetings with Jim, the chancellor, and at a mixer with several prominent ASU alumni. After all the meetings, I flew straight back to Arkansas. I tried to describe Boone and Appalachian State as best I could to Margaret. We had to practice pronouncing App-uh-latch-un before we went back. It was important to pronounce it like the local folks did. If you called it Appalay-shan, you stood out as an outsider. We got it right, though.*

Margaret: *Jerry and I decided to drive back up to Boone to look it over without telling anyone we were coming. We left that weekend and drove straight through in 13 hours. It was a cold and overcast late February morning. Dirty snow was piled up on the shoulder of Highway 105 as we entered town. Unlike Jerry, I'm afraid my first impression of the city wasn't very good. Boone was so small and planted right in the middle of the mountains. That took some getting used to, but I knew that Jerry wanted to take the job, and I knew we would be happy there. He would be a head coach again.*

Boone, as Margaret and Jerry learned, was located in the heart of the ancient and beautiful Appalachian Mountains. As its name indicated, the town was named after the fabled frontiersman Daniel Boone, who explored and hunted the region in the 1760s. Legend has it that he camped in an area that is now downtown Boone.

Watauga County was formed in 1849, and Boone, with a population of 150, was incorporated in that same year. The tiny town lay isolated in a small valley of the Blue Ridge Mountains of the Appalachian chain. Beset by harsh winters and lack of roads and railroads, not many settlers were attracted to the area.

In 1899, one of Boone's leading citizens, Daniel Baker Dougherty, convinced the town it needed a school to educate the mountain people. He and J. F. Hardin raised $1,000 and donated land to build the Watauga Academy. Daniel Baker Doughtery's two sons, Dauphin Disco Dougherty and Blanfort Barnard Dougherty, returned home to act as co-principals.

Photograph by Dick Brown

The fabled frontiersman Daniel Boone was reported to have camped in what is now downtown Boone. In a tribute to the town's namesake, a life-size statue of Boone and his dogs, resting around a campfire, sits on the beautiful Applachian State campus.

From that humble beginning against all the odds of bad weather, isolation, and meager finances, an educational institution was launched. It struggled through many changes and grew into what is now Appalachian State University.

While teacher training was the primary legacy of the Doughertys, expansion into other disciplines was inevitable. By 1967, Appalachian State Teachers College had blossomed into a regional university offering over 30 degree programs; it joined the greater University of North Carolina system in 1971.

The consistent recognition of Appalachian as one of the leading educational institutions in the country by such prestigious magazines as *Time* and *Newsweek* has attracted students from states outside of North Carolina and around the world.

Boone loved its Mountaineers, and being outnumbered by the university student body almost since its beginning had never bothered the local townspeople. Maybe that was partly because Appalachian State University was the largest employer in the region. Or they just simply loved their Mountaineers.

In addition to high national academic ratings, athletics had also attracted young student athletes to the campus shoehorned into the hills surrounding Boone. The long winning tradition of the Mountaineer football team had drawn national attention on ESPN Sports television each season. Faithful students and fans had made Appalachian State a leader in the Southern Conference in home attendance.

Jerry and Margaret twisted and turned on the mountainous highway for hours in the dark mist of night that covered them like a large, wet blanket. Finally the rising sun filtered through tall pine trees that lined the craggy embankments, giving way to morning. Daylight was welcomed by the Moores, even if it brought with it the sight of dirty melting snow along the side of the highway from a recent winter snowstorm.

Jerry's eyes surveyed the town as they turned off N.C. 105 onto U.S. 421. They entered town and U.S. 421 became King Street, the main thoroughfare of the business district. They drove past old buildings that had been renovated into restaurants and clothing stores to serve the university students that outnumbered the town population of 12,000. There were also the typical small-town insurance offices and law offices clustered around the courthouse that served Watauga County.

They pulled into town and waited for the businesses to come to life. The chamber of commerce was their first stop for coffee and information.

Boone, they learned, rested at an elevation of 3,333 feet and averaged three feet of snow a year. Cold wind and snow were no problem. Wind continually swept the cap-rock plains of Lubbock. The temperature in Lubbock equaled the average 35-degree winter temperatures of Boone. Five years in Nebraska had hardened them against bitter winters that were long and harsh. The relatively cool Appalachian summers of 70 degrees definitely would not be a problem. In East Texas that was considered a cold front.

Mast General Store caught their attention, with its turn-of-the-century charm and the unique, hard-to-find items that filled its shelves. It reminded them of the quaint shops in their small hometowns back in Texas.

The Appalachian State campus was visible from King Street as they continued their loop around downtown to Rivers Street.

"Let's go check out the football stadium," Jerry said when they reached Stadium Drive.

Jerry nosed the car up the steep incline toward Kidd Brewer Stadium. The playing field was blocked from view by Owens Field House. Jerry reckoned it was the largest flat space in Boone. The bleachers crowded against a stone wall on the west side and the south end zone's grassy bank was ringed by trees. The stadium looked like it had been chiseled out of the side of the millenniums-old mountainside. It was a far cry from Jones Stadium at Texas Tech and Nebraska's stadium in Lincoln that held 80,000 fans.

"Looks like it might hold 15,000," Jerry observed. "Kind of small compared to what we're used to. At least the playing field's the same size," he chuckled as he headed out of the campus.

"I guess we've seen all we need to see. Are you ready to find someplace for a bite of lunch?" he asked Margaret.

They pulled into the gravel parking lot of the large white-frame colonial-style Dan'l Boone Inn. The neatly appointed Southern-style restaurant was a restful retreat for the two weary travelers. After a quiet lunch, Margaret and Jerry climbed back into their car and headed back home to Arkansas.

"Well, it is pretty small," Margaret said.

"What is?"

"Everything, and it's a long way from the kids," she added, as if she might be trying to talk Jerry out of the "opportunity" Jim Garner had offered him.

"They're a Division I team, but AA," Jerry said, as if thinking out loud. "Sparky Woods had winners every year and was in the play-offs four out of five years. The school has a long winning tradition." Jerry sounded like his confidence was slipping again. He turned to Margaret. "What do you think?"

"I've seen places I'd rather live. But we both grew up in small towns. I think it has potential, and this is your chance to be a head coach again. Maybe this division is right for you. If you want the job, then we'll become Mountaineers. Remember the leap of faith we took going to Arkansas as a volunteer? That worked out, didn't it?"

Exhausted from the nonstop round trip to Boone, they arrived home about the time they usually were getting up. They fell into bed and when they woke up they had slept through church. Jerry put on a pot of coffee. Their muscles were aching from being cooped up in a car for too long.

The steaming coffee seemed to chase away the cobwebs left from the events of the last 48 hours. Jerry sipped from his cup and looked across the table at Margaret.

"I'm going to call Jim," he said, as he slowly rose from the breakfast table and sauntered over toward the kitchen wall phone.

"I knew you wanted that job the minute Jim offered it to you, sight unseen. After visiting Boone and checking out the campus, it was a foregone conclusion. Go ahead, call him, and let's get this show on the road."

"Hello, Jim, this is Jerry. I hate to bother you at home, but if that job offer is still good, I'll take it. Margaret and I drove up and back this weekend. I think Appalachian will be a good fit for us."

The conversation was short. "He wants me up there right away," Jerry said. "I need to hire my assistant coaches and get to know the players before spring practice in only a couple of weeks." He waited for a response from Margaret, knowing that meant they would be separated again for a while.

"That's fine, you go on ahead; I'll be okay. I have to finish out the year teaching then I'll join you in May. It's only three months."

George Tharell, Jerry's good friend and spiritual mentor in Arkansas, said it best: "His faith is the thing that sustained him during these last few years. God opened up the door at Appalachian State after closing it at Texas Tech."

Margaret: *We had prayed about it and felt God was answering our prayers. Jerry was a different man almost overnight after the job offer at Appalachian State. He had had a wonderful experience at Arkansas. Coach Hatfield was a fine Christian and family man. He was a good friend to Jerry and considerate of his staff. Jerry learned from Ken how he would treat his new staff. He wanted them to have time away from the practice field to spend with their families.*

Jerry had made up his mind in Fayetteville that if given another chance to be a head coach, he wasn't going to hold anything back in the boldness of his faith. That if God saw to it that He wanted to put him back into coaching, it would be because He wanted Jerry to make a difference in the spiritual lives of the kids he coached. He doesn't push it on anybody. He just sets such a fine example they can see the Lord shining through him.

CLIMBING BACK UP
THE MOUNTAIN

Jerry: *I packed a few things and went right back to Boone Monday morning. A press conference was scheduled for Saturday. There were some upset fans over the way Sparky Woods left so abruptly, and we expected that. We've been in these situations before; it just comes with the job.*

I got a late start and wanted to get my coaches hired and meet the players before spring practice started. There wasn't any time to recruit. I had to go with what Sparky had recruited. Fortunately, he and his staff had done an excellent job and had recruited some really good athletes.

Asheville, North Carolina

A press conference was scheduled for March 4 at the Asheville Civic Center in the overcast Smoky Mountains. Athletic Director Jim Garner called the media together to announce the hiring of Jerry Moore as the new head coach of the Appalachian State Mountaineers football team. Garner was well aware of the doubts and questions many ASU fans had expressed over the poor record Moore had as a head coach.

The mountains were still clinging to the colder weather with the temperatures in the 40s before the sun burned off the morning mountain fog to let in a little warmth.

Appalachian fans were accustomed to a winning team that made the play-offs almost every year in pursuit of a national championship. Sparky Woods had won Coach of the Year three times, and five winning seasons left fans hungry for more.

Having to drive in lingering fog didn't help the frame of mind of the fans that had come to find out just who this Texan was. The audience looked for assurances from both Moore and Jim Garner that the Mountaineers' winning tradition was going to continue. The tension hung in the civic center like the low-ceiling clouds that brought the cold front to the mountains. Both men put on their best press conference faces and stepped up to face an anxious crowd.

"Good morning and welcome. It's good to see so many familiar faces. For those who don't know me, I'm Jim Garner, athletic director of Appalachian State University. As you know, we're all here to meet and greet the new coach of the Appalachian State Mountaineers football team. There has been some talk going around about hiring a friend with a losing record as head coach." Garner paused and took a sip of water as he tried to measure the crowd's response.

A drink of water this early in his introduction was a sure sign of nervousness, which he had hidden very well until now.

"You can rest assured," he said, "that I've never hired a coach based on wins and losses. ASU basketball coach Tom Apke wasn't a winnner at Colorado with a record of 59-81. But look what he's doing now, 20-8 this season."

That short analysis took some of the edge off the crowd's emotions, but they wanted more assurance than that.

"In a coach we look for people of high integrity who are academically oriented and are fun to be around. After those things, we try to hire the best coach we can find," he said with a smile.

"Yes, I've known Jerry Moore for over 20 years through different jobs at a couple of different schools. But we've not been bosom buddies," Garner said. "I didn't hire him out of friendship. I believe he's the man to take an already good program to the next level."

With that closing statement Garner stepped back from the podium and extended his right arm towards Moore, seated behind him. "Ladies and gentlemen, I present Jerry Moore, the new Appalachian State head football coach."

Cautious but polite applause met Coach Moore, who approached the microphone in his slow Texas gait. He grasped the podium with both hands and held his head high as he faced the crowd. If he was nervous it didn't show. Moore dipped his head slightly to acknowledge their applause. Without further hesitation, he got right to the heart of the occasion.

"I am honored to be the coach at Appalachian State. You have a wonderful tradition here and I intend to continue that tradition and graduate fine young athletes, students, and men prepared to meet the challenges of the world.

"At North Texas, 10 of our 11 loses were to bowl teams. That's what kept the budget going. At Texas Tech, 17 of our losses were by less than a touchdown." He looked straight into the audience and continued. "I could stand up here and make excuses all day for every ball game. At that time, the Southwest Conference was probably the toughest conference in America. But the fact is we got beat."

The local press had played up the fact that Woods had boasted his best team ever would be in 1989. That was before he announced he was leaving. The question in everyone's mind was, could Moore live up to Woods' prediction?

"I hope Coach Woods is right about his prediction," Moore said, acknowledging the oft-quoted remark by Woods. "There shouldn't be that much of a transition offensively or defensively. We'll basically be a multiple I-formation football team. We may be a little more option-oriented than ASU has been, if we have the people to do that."

He eased his grip on the podium and met the rumors head-on.

"In any profession you have to prove yourself every day; I don't mind proving myself to Appalachian State. We want to make everyone proud of the way we handle our business on and off the field."

The audience liked Moore's friendly, folksy manner and confidence. But not everyone was convinced he could deliver on his promises. He had given up a lucrative business venture in Texas making several times his salary at ASU.

Instead of the prosperous and secure business world, Moore was once again involved with the sport he loved as a head football coach.

He responded to the first question by a *Charlotte Observer* reporter, who asked why he was willing to give up his lucrative career in Texas to coach a Division I-AA team.

"I liked the newness of it," he said, referring to his job in Dallas. "I liked the challenge of it and it didn't hurt that I was making a lot of money." The crowd broke into laughter, dispelling the tension that had hung over the room since the beginning.

"But when the season got under way, I was missing it. I started going to games up at Clemson. After about a year, I knew it was time to get back into coaching. My daughter had graduated from high school, the main reason we kept the homeplace in Lubbock. I knew that all I wanted to do was coach football no matter where I had to go. And here I am."

Then the inevitable question came. "Do you think you will be able to match Coach Woods record of two conference championships and three Coach of the Year awards in five winning seasons?"

"Woods will be a tough act to follow, no question about it, but I haven't given it much thought. In this business it doesn't matter what the guy before you did. If you don't win, you're out. What Sparky did was his accomplishment. What we do will be ours."

Showing no signs of pressure, Jerry had calmly faced and won over his audience. Now all he had to do was hire a coaching staff before the end of spring break on March 14, in time to meet the team for the first time.

> Jerry: *I was a lot smarter when I came to Appalachian than when I went to Texas Tech. I hired some coaches that probably should have been head coach instead of me. In five years I had met a lot of good coaches and made a lot of contacts. And it was a good thing, because I had to build a staff in just a couple of weeks. This was my first experience in I-AA ball. But I was lucky to have a good recruit class coming in and some good experienced players that stayed when so many went with Sparky to South Carolina.*
>
> *All the coaches I knew were from Texas. I called on friends for recommendations and Danny Ford gave me a really good one in Ruffin McNeill. He gave our staff a tremendous boost because he was a good defensive coach at East Carolina and had recruiting experience in this area.*

THE TEXAS MAFIA

Jerry: *It was only a couple of weeks before spring practice when they hired me. I needed to get my staff together in a hurry, but I wanted to do it right and get the right chemistry. I didn't have them all hired until the day before our first team meeting. Because most of us were from Texas, we were nicknamed the Texas Mafia. The fans and press had some fun with that.*

By the time fall practice started, 52 players from the 1988 team had left. Quite a few followed Sparky [Woods] to South Carolina. Some just got discouraged and quit the program. A few had academic problems and others just didn't show up for whatever reason. I don't think it was anything against us. They just felt jilted or abandoned when Sparky left. There was a lot of stress; it was like a revolving door.

When I first got here, to be honest, down deep, I didn't think I'd be here very long. The coaches' locker room was like a closet and we had no meeting rooms. The facilities just weren't adequate at that time. But a building program soon upgraded the facility to one of the finest around.

After so many players left, there was some concern about the team, but we had a solid core of veterans, and Sparky had signed some really good recruits that stayed with us. We had some athletes who wanted to play football. We finished 9-3 that season and made the play-offs.

Jerry Moore was greeted with caution by many fans and alumni. His losing record at Texas Tech was a hard fact for many to overlook, even though he had engineered the powerful Nebraska team as offensive coordinator for six bowl trips while he was there. His short tenure at Arkansas saw them go to bowl games with Moore on the sidelines as receivers' coach and assistant offensive coordinator.

But Jerry didn't let what other people thought bother him. He met his new audience as an open and honest man who truly believed he could produce winning football teams at Appalachian. His folksy Texan manner and dry sense of humor played well with the fans. He also convinced them he was as much interested in building young men's character and academics as he was in producing good athletes.

Doubts and constant press comparisons of his losing record as a head coach against Sparky Woods' winning record at ASU didn't phase Jerry. He was back doing what he always wanted to do and that's all that mattered to him. He quickly assembled his new staff. Less than two weeks after being hired, Coach Jerry Moore called a press conference.

"I would like to announce my new assistant coaches. We have all worked together before or knew each other as coaches in the Southwest Conference, with a couple of exceptions. Rob Best coached the offensive line at Texas Tech. David Browning coached the Texas A&M line for 17 years. Danny Nutt was an assistant with me at Arkansas and coached the receivers. Blake Feldt played his college ball at Texas Tech and was coaching at University of Texas. John Wiley played his college ball at East Texas State and was coaching defensive backs at the University of Texas. Ruffin McNeill, defensive coach, comes to us from East Carolina. They are all good coaches and are as dedicated as I am to the future excellence of Appalachian State football."

The fact that most of his new assistants were from Texas wasn't lost on the crowd, especially the news media.

A reporter from the *Banner* asked immediately after the announcement, "Coach, just how many of your coaches are from Texas?"

"All but Ruffin McNeill and Danny Nutt. In any business, you work with the people you know best and have a good relationship with. Football is no different. These are all good men and good coaches I've known for several years. Where they come from doesn't matter to me. Danny and I coached together at Arkansas. Ruffin McNeill isn't from Texas, but he's a good coach. He was recommended to me by my good friend Danny Ford.

"Ruff did a great job at East Carolina and will be a great asset to this program. My interest is in building a good staff that can continue the excellent football program at Appalachian. That's what I looked for. I took my time on this, since I had almost two weeks." He smiled and got a good laugh from the reporters. "I wanted to get it right. I feel good about this. I've got a very positive feeling, a lot of positive vibes."

A reporter in the group said, "It looks like we've been invaded by the Texas Mafia."

After the audience laughter died down, Moore in his dry wit said, "Well, if that's what it takes, then I guess you have." Another round of laughter greeted his retort and the crowd dispersed, laughing and commenting about the new Texas posse that had arrived in Boone.

> Jerry: *I brought nearly a dozen pairs of the finest Western boots you have ever seen up here. But I never wore them. Not because of all that Texas Mafia stuff. I just didn't want to rub it in. I had to prove myself as coach of the Appalachian football team and not flaunt my Texas background. I wasn't a Texan anymore, I was a Mountaineer.*

The jokes about the Texas Mafia disappeared as did the constant comparisons of Moore's and Woods' records from fans and the local sports pages.

> Margaret: *I didn't get up to Boone until the end of May after school was out. I was under contract and didn't want to break my contract in mid-semester. Coach Ken Hatfield had gone to bat for me to get that job. I had good credentials, but there were a lot of good teachers out there that needed a job. I didn't want to ruin it for the next coach that came along whose wife needed a teaching job.*
>
> *It was really hard at first. We lived in a motel for a few*

weeks, then moved into a married students' apartment for a short while, then moved to a really nice house in Blowing Rock. When the summer season came, the lease went up really high for tourist rates and we didn't want to pay that much.

Dr. Richard Furman came to our rescue. He and Jerry had become good friends and he was Jerry's spiritual mentor. In fact, they became such close friends that they started a fellowship get-together on a small lake on his property. The informal gathering was attended by the coaches and any players that wanted to come on Wednesday nights. It was a great time of just a bunch of guys eating around a big firepit, enjoying fellowship. They prayed and shared personal stories with the group. They continue to meet to this day.

Anyway, back to our housing dilemma. Doctor Furman had a log house on his property and let us move in for the rest of that summer until the rates went down again. We were going to move back into the house in Blowing Rock, but Dick Furman said we could just stay there until we sold our dream house in Texas.

We had some good times in that log cabin. We got snowed in during the blizzard in 1991 and were stuck there for five or six days. When we tried to get out, the snow was waist deep. We couldn't even get up to the Furmans' house just up the hill above us. Lots of people were stranded and helicopters had to drop hay for the cattle. We survived though. There was plenty of food; I had books to read and our little TV got three stations.

It took us two and a half years to sell our house in Texas. By then we were more than ready to leave the cabin. It was quite an experience, but we had fun.

Being unsettled and so far away from their family made those first few years hard for the Moores, especially Margaret. It was their first time without the children being close.

What Jerry Moore didn't expect when he arrived at Appalachian was for half of his team to quit before they ever played a single game for him. That was a mutiny of proportions that had never been seen before in school history, not at Appalachian, not anywhere.

Things looked pretty bleak when fall practice started. Fifty-two players had left the program. The expected starting quarterback from the previous year's team, Bobby Fuller, was among those players who followed Sparky Woods to South Carolina. Fuller's backup, Lance Redding, who was the only experienced quarterback left in camp, ran into grade problems and was ruled academically ineligible.

Margaret: *Jerry was concerned, but he didn't get upset with those players. He certainly didn't want them here if they didn't want to be. Most had left before we got here, but several left after spring practice. He worked the dog out of them. His work ethic was different than Sparky's, and some quit for that reason. I can tell you that many of the ones that left came back later and told Jerry it was the biggest mistake of their lives.*

It could have been bad with all those guys quitting, but Jerry isn't one to rant and rave about something; he's just going to accept it and make it better if he can.

Jerry: *I guess it could have been worse. But after watching D. J. Campbell work out in fall practice, I knew we were in good shape at quarterback. He just got better and better each week. He had great instincts, could run, and had a strong passing arm. Just an all-around good athlete and he played well for us.*

NEW ERA BEGINS AT
APPALACHIAN STATE

Jerry: There was a lot of pressure that first year. Looking back now, I'm amazed at the season we had. I didn't think anything else could go wrong before our first game that hadn't already happened. We took a small core of veterans that were still there and played a lot of young players. Our first game really told us what kind of team we had. I think we surprised everybody.

Owens Field House locker room—September 2, 1989

"All right, listen up. We'll be facing our first big test in a few minutes. You've worked hard and we are depending on a lot of you young players. But let me tell you something."

Coach Moore launched into his favorite motivational speech. "My freshman year when I was playing high school ball back in Bonham, Texas, we had great talent, but we didn't win a single game. The next year we changed coaches and he taught us how to work hard and believe in ourselves. We didn't have the best talent, but we didn't lose a regular-season game after that. Now you've got the talent and the desire to win. Let's go out there and see what we are made of. Do we have the desire to win?"

Photograph by Keith Cline/ASU Athletics

The Appalachian State football team pats this plaque for good luck as
they pass through the locker-room door before each game.

A resounding yes echoed off the shiny yellow cinder-block walls
as the team roared out of the dressing room and slapped a plaque over
the locker-room door.

The black plaque in the shape of the state of North Carolina
had a slogan across the middle: "Today I give my ALL for Appalachian
State." Worn from many seasons of pregame slaps, the old plaque
shuddered with each hit but never failed the black-and-gold warriors
passing by. It was an old tradition that also made all the road games.

More than 12,000 students and loyal fans showed up to see their
new coach in action. They were curious about how he and the team
would respond to the adversity of losing so many players after Sparky
Woods' sudden departure. Expectations were high and the tailgate
parties before game time were abuzz with apprehension. How a bunch
of freshmen would be able to compete in the tough Southern Conference was on everyone's mind.

Appalachian opened the 1989 season at home with a thrashing
of Gardner-Webb, 43-7. The Mountaineers traveled to Winston-Salem
after a week of hard practice, the same preparation they did every

week, no matter who their next opponent was. Quarterback D. J. Campbell, with his first win under his belt, teamed up with veteran tailback Ritchie Melchor and sliced up the Wake Forest defense for a 15-10 victory. The team came of age against an upper-division foe and set the tone for the rest of the season.

The Jerry Moore era was under way in the High Country. Appalachian fans were giddy with the results of their new coach and any doubts about his ability to win were forgotten.

The Mountaineers plowed through their schedule feeding on each win to carry them through the next week. Their only losses were to archrivals The Citadel and Furman. Their 9-2 record, undefeated on their home field, was good enough to put them in the play-offs.

The only scholarship quarterback left on the roster was a lanky 6-2, 180-pound freshman named D. J. Campbell from Cleveland, Georgia. Campbell was highly recruited as a versatile three-sport star in high school by Georgia Tech and Furman, as well as Appalachian.

Campbell was unfazed at being thrown into a starting role as a true freshman. He improved with each game and carried the Mountaineers to the Southern Conference play-offs. A disappointing loss in the first round to Middle Tennessee State by a field goal ended an otherwise successful season for the Mountaineers.

There was no longer any question that athletic director Jim Garner had made the right choice in hiring Jerry Moore. A 9-3 overall record with six home wins made Moore only the second Mountaineer head coach in 43 years to post nine victories in his first season. A seventh-place finish in Division I-AA ranking was the final reward for Moore, who took a young team of mostly freshmen and sophomores against all odds and made them winners.

Coach Moore and his band of underclassmen had accomplished the impossible. Sadly, the euphoria didn't last past the first round in the play-offs. Had they beaten Furman and won home-field advantage by winning the conference championship, everyone felt they would have advanced further in the play-offs, but it wasn't to be. It didn't really matter; once-questioning fans were now ardent supporters of Jerry Moore. Some even said his first season was a miracle. It would be the first of many more to come on Moore's watch.

Although the miracle season came to a disappointing end, thousands of black-and-gold faithful were already thinking about next year.

They now had an unshakable confidence in their new coach and young team that would only get better in the coming seasons.

In the postgame interview after their play-off loss, the usually mild-mannered Jerry Moore was still livid over the officiating of the game. A questionable non-call in the final quarter helped Middle Tennessee score the tying touchdown. With only six seconds on the clock, a gut-wrenching field goal pulled the game out for the Blue Raiders of Middle Tennessee State, 24-21.

"I have been coaching longer than any of these kids have been living," said the 50-year-old Moore, "and I've never seen more indecisive calls in a game. I was shocked by the way the game was called."

"In my 27 years of coaching, I've never commented on officiating," he said. "But it's hard not to focus on the way this game was officiated."

> Jerry: *It was a tough loss. Those officials were really awful. Missed calls and bad calls, stuff like that really had our guys upset, but that was no excuse for losing our composure. We should have won that game, but we let it get away from us. We knew we were a better team than that and that this was just the beginning of better things to come. Those young players worked hard and matured under fire, showing a strong belief that they could win, and then went out and did it on the playing field. There was some disappointment at how it ended, but it was a really good season. They gained a lot of experience and developed character from it. They came a long way, especially after the way it started out with half the team quitting.*
>
> *All the preseason questions were answered by the Gardner-Webb game. Those young men played their hearts out. Ritchie Melchor, our senior tailback, was terrific for us. And I can't say enough about our freshman quarterback, D. J. Campbell. Those young players were our foundation for the next three seasons.*

THROWN FOR A LOSS

Jerry: *We had a lot of injuries to key people in '93. Our preseason ranking was No. 18 in the nation. That was based on our previous 7-5 season and second consecutive trip to the play-offs. I've never paid any attention to polls. They are just for talking. It's good for the fans, alumni, and everybody to talk about, but that stuff doesn't mean a thing. We proved that in '93. It was my first and only losing season at Appalachian. We just couldn't keep our guys healthy until toward the end of the season when the veterans got back in the game and our walk-on quarterback, Scott Satterfield, had learned his job under fire.*

Along with the injuries, we were a young football team. Sometimes you look up and see you have 18 seniors playing for you and some of those are backups for the starters. That's what happened to us in '92, so recruiting was part of it.

Sure, there were some really unhappy fans because of our 4-7 record. The good that came out of it was they developed into a good football team. We got better each week and won our last three games, including beating a good Western Carolina team that we probably knocked out of a chance to go to the play-offs.

What most people don't realize is that same team got better in '94 and was a really good team in '95.

Yeah, some people wanted me fired, but I didn't think much about it. I didn't read the papers or listen to the sports news. They have a right to their opinions and can say anything they want to, but I can't pay attention to that kind of stuff. That's somebody else's problem. My job is to coach the football team and that's what I do to the best of my ability.

I didn't blame the coaches; I put it all on me. As soon as that season was over, all the coaches sat down to work it out and fix what went wrong. There wasn't much we could do about injuries; they're part of the game. You just have to have everybody ready to step in anytime they're needed and that's what we did beginning with 6:00 A.M. workouts in March of '94. We used to do those morning workouts every spring and just kind of let it slip when we came here. We started them up again, and everyone recommitted themselves to football—even the coaches. It paid off.

Expectations were mounting in the High Country when fall colors covered the beautiful Blue Ridge Mountains and Mountaineer football arrived. A returning veteran team from the previous year's 7-5 play-off team had everyone pumped up. Would this be their year for a championship? Fans and alumni were happy with the almost yearly play-off appearances, but a groundswell for more was building up. They wanted a national championship, something that had never been accomplished before.

But then, fall practice happened. Veteran players were falling like pine trees in an ice storm.

Jerry: *We had some big holes on both sides of the line. When D. J. Campbell left there were some big shoes to fill at quarterback. He had started all 47 games in his four years at Appalachian, so we didn't have any experienced quarterbacks. Our starter was supposed to be senior Andy Arnold, who had played behind D. J. for three years. He broke his collarbone in fall practice and we had to go with third-string red-shirt sophomore walk-on Scott Satterfield and a lot of freshmen. It was like starting all over, like we did in '89.*

Scott Satterfield was an untested 190-pound right-hander who could run and throw. Although his passing record for the only two games he had played in was a paltry 0-1, he had impressed Moore and his offensive coordinator, Rob Best, enough to put him on scholarship by his sophomore year.

Announcing Satterfield as the starting quarterback in a press interview, Moore spoke highly of his untried quarterback. He masked any concerns he may have held privately about the walk-on starter's abilities to do the job.

"I have a high level of confidence in Scott," Moore said. "Over the last couple of seasons he's shown some elusiveness and ability to make plays. We like our quarterbacks to be able to do it all. We run some options, sprint-outs, we drop back. Scott has shown all those things."

Going into a tough four-game nonconference schedule on the road with a third-string quarterback and without six other injured starters in the line, put a lot of pressure on the young makeshift Mountaineers. The long road trips were a disaster. ASU lost four straight before coming home to the more friendly surroundings of Kidd Brewer Stadium. It was the worst start in the history of Appalachian football.

Home-field turf with the stadium full of anxious, noisy fans gave the patched-up team the confidence they needed. The faithful fans wanted a win as badly as the players did. They weren't accustomed to watching their team lose and seemed to be cheering extra loud for their wounded black-and-gold warriors' first home game.

Speaking to a pregame press conference, Coach Moore said, "There's no way we'll know how our young kids are going to react in front of the home crowd. Seven of our 22 starters are playing their first college game of their lives. But I feel like we have a prepared football team. They've learned a lot from those losses. We just have to put those games behind us and play our best ball. Coach Feldt has his guys on the line as prepared as you can have a group of freshmen. They've worked hard and improved every week. I guarantee you they are giving their best effort every snap of the ball."

All their hard work and boisterous home-team fan support helped the Mountaineers gut out a 20-16 win over East Tennessee State for their first win in five games. In addition to winning their first game of the season, the Apps upheld their tradition of being a tough team to beat at Kidd Brewer Stadium. Jubilant fans showered their team with praise and felt that they had rounded the corner, and the season was back on track.

The Mountaineers had improved their play. Touchdown production was up with tailback Chip Hooks leading the ground game. Freshman linebacker Dexter Coakley took over as the team's leading tackler. But the excitement of High Country fans and alumni didn't last long. Sadly the improvement wasn't enough to break out of their losing slump. The Mountaineers went to 1-7 with no hope of getting to the play-offs.

"We had some youth issues on offense and some transition issues on defense," said veteran assistant John Wiley. "But we had a real strong freshman class. One game I was in the press box, and defensive coordinator Ruffin McNeill was down on the sidelines. We were talking and he said, 'Yote [short for coyote, his nickname for Wiley], I'm looking at some of the best defensive players standing over here on the sideline.'

"We were running two systems, a hybrid system of what he had done at East Carolina with an eight-man front that was the standard for years. I had left for a couple of years when Coach Moore called me back to coach the secondary. I brought some four-front stuff from Valdosta State that most of the country was using at that time. After converting to the four-three, it became the permanent basis of our defense."

The Mountaineers got their second wind and started building momentum late in the season with wins over Tennessee-Chattanooga and Western Carolina. In beating Western Carolina, they kept the coveted Old Mountain Jug—a tradition started in 1976 that awarded a specially engraved jug to the winner of the annual rivalry that came to be known as the Jug Game. The Jug had left Boone only twice since Coach Jerry Moore arrived in 1989.

With two straight wins under their belts, the inspired Mountaineers headed to Lexington, Virginia, to meet VMI. It had been a frustrating year and the battle-seasoned young team took it out on VMI. ASU overpowered the Keydets with a convincing 35-21 victory. It ended the Mountaineers' first losing season since 1984 on a positive note.

It was a long and painful season. In spite of the dismal record, the hard work of Coach Moore and his staff in rebuilding an injury-riddled team manned mostly by untried underclassman didn't go unnoticed.

"I've often said that was one of Coach Moore's best coaching jobs I have ever witnessed in all the years we've been coaching together," longtime assistant Wiley said. "We started out 1-7 that year and Coach did a tremendous job on the practice field not letting players get down and keeping the coaches motivated. That motivation helped us win our last three games and led us through the '94 and '95 seasons."

Six Mountaineers were honored by the Southern Conference. Junior tailback Chip Hooks was voted first team. Dexter Coakley (future NFL All-Pro for the Dallas Cowboys), who set a new Appalachian freshman record with 146 tackles, was voted Southern Conference Freshman of the Year.

While many disgruntled fans and alumni were calling for Coach Moore's job, Jerry was unfazed by the criticism and mean-spirited things fans had said about his ability to coach. Instead, he was positive about the future of his ball club in a postgame interview after the VMI win.

"Our players worked hard for this win in spite of a bad season," Moore said. "We grew as a team and learned to work together as a team with a lot of young players stepping up to the challenge. We learned to trust and depend on each other to overcome a lot of adversity. I have learned that sometimes there has to be adversity in order to move forward, and I think that's what we did. We will be a better team for it."

A couple of months later, Coach Moore addressed his staff, players, alumni, and fans at the annual sports banquet honoring ASU athletes.

"This year was my fault. I shoulder every bit of the responsibility, and I don't want to go through another year like this year. I don't want to go through it for myself; I don't want to go through it for our players, or for the people that care about our football program.

"Personally I am more excited about recruiting than I've ever been; I'm more excited about spring practice and about what is ahead of us. I can't put my finger on why I feel this way; it's just a feeling I have inside. I can't wait for next season to start."

Margaret: Jerry's demeanor didn't change during the losing season. That just wasn't Jerry. I don't know what he did at practice, but he was the same around here when he came home at night. In fact, Andy Matthews, a team trainer, told me that Jerry coached better when his back was against the wall.

Later in 2005 Andy was sitting behind us at the semifinal game against Furman. I turned and said, "Coach's back is against the wall." He smiled back, nodded his head, and replied, "Yep." We beat Furman and went on to win our first national championship.

No, Jerry doesn't let things get to him anymore. Those two years after he was fired from Texas Tech, we drew closer to each other and the Lord. His faith is really strong.

THE ALMOST
PERFECT SEASON

Jerry: *I really thought we would go the distance in 1995. The conference was tough that year and we played some strong nonconference teams. Those Texas teams are always tough, but I didn't think anybody could knock us off the ball the way Stephen F. Austin did in the play-offs. The big difference in that game was their ability to run the football and our inability to run the football. Their defense was awesome against our offense. They held Damon Scott, one of the best runners we've ever had, to 16 yards and that took us out of our game plan. But we thought we had it locked up. We played hard, but they outsmarted us at the end of the game and took home a win.*

Margaret: *Jerry wouldn't say this, but I didn't think that team was as talented as some we've had. They just played hard together and had great chemistry. It was one of those years when everything pulled together. That's the class that comes back the most. They love to come back and have a good time and swap stories. They come back because they love it and are dedicated to Jerry and Appalachian State. A few make it to the pros, but that isn't the reason most players come here. Unlike the bigger schools,*

whose players see school as their ticket to the NFL, these kids
come where they are taught discipline and the team concept. Jerry
and his coaches are strict and don't put up with any foolishness.
They are just as concerned about the kind of person their players
are on and off the playing field. He tries to prepare them for life in
the outside world physically, spiritually, and academically.

Owens Field House—1995

The Yosef Club's reception room in Owens Field House was
crowded with reporters. They had grazed over several tables of finger
foods, chips, dips, and an unending supply of diet sodas and bottled
water, waiting for Coach Moore. Jerry traditionally ate the pregame
meal with the team in the athletic dorm's cafeteria and walked up the
hill with the team to the field house.

An Associated Press reporter yelled from the back of the cluster
of reporters gathered in front of Jerry's podium. "What was the key to
an undefeated season this year, Coach?"

"We learned a lot of lessons from the 4-7 season two years ago.
It opened my eyes to some things. We went back to an old format, to
even when I was a high school coach, of spending more time with the
players," he said.

"Coaches and programs have gotten so specialized. There was a
time in my career as a high school coach you would tape those kids'
ankles—you were the coach, the equipment man, and everything. After the 1993 season I told my coaches we weren't as attached or close
to our players as we needed to be.

"We started spending a lot more time with our players as coaches. We weren't around our players enough; that was my point."

"What coaching strategies or personnel changes did you make?"
a Watauga Democrat reporter questioned from the front row.

"Like I said, after the 1993 disaster, both the coaching staff and
players recommitted themselves to football." With a grin he said,
"Then there were those 6:00 A.M. off-season workouts we started up
again. We had done that several years ago but kind of dropped it. Well,
now we have full attendance by players and coaches to show they are
working for a common goal. The same is true of our summer strength-
workout program."

KING OF THE MOUNTAIN

"What about your Texas connection? Most of your staff came from there, and your son Chris, a student assistant, actually played at Stephen F. Austin. How's it going to feel playing them?"

Jerry grinned again, straightened his black baseball-style hat with a big gold A emblazoned on it, and answered, "For me there's no mystique about playing a school from Texas. It's been ten years since I've been in Texas as a coach.

"I've known SFA's coach, John Pearce, since he was a high school coach," he said. "He's a good football coach and he's always been associated with good football programs. We prepared for them just like we always do for every team we've played; they're no different."

A voice from the back of the group shouted over the clatter of questions fired at the coach. "Will your No. 2 national ranking help your players' efforts in the play-offs?"

Moore shook his head. "I've always said polls don't mean a thing. That stuff's just for you guys to write about. Don't misunderstand, we feel good about being ranked No. 2, but we don't talk about it much during the season. When players strap on their helmets week after week and go after each other and come out a winner, that means something. Unlike the other division, we decide who is No. 1 on the playing field, not by who gets the most votes."

Jerry's jab at Division I teams, who play bowl games and are voted on as to who the No. 1 team is, brought a ripple of laughter from the media scribes. It has always been a point of pride in Division I-AA that the teams have a play-off system and can rightly claim they are No. 1 when they are the last team standing.

Moore went on to describe similarities between the two teams and their records and offered the usual tributes opposing coaches pay each other before a big game.

Jerry held up his arms to signal the end of the press conference. "You've done your job; now I have to go do mine," he said and left the podium to join his team, preparing to meet Stephen F. Austin for what they hoped would be another win to advance to the semifinal round.

In the locker room before the kickoff, Moore gathered his team around him. "Men, we've come a long way from our worst season ever. You've worked hard, grown up as athletes and young men. You know what it feels like to trust one another, believe in yourselves, and play with a will to win. There's nothing else I can say to you now. Just go out there and play the game with all your heart! Let's go!"

Whooping and yelling, the team charged through the large inflated-helmet archway, past the spewing white fireworks, and into the cold December night air. They were fired up and didn't feel the 30 degree temperature as they were greeted by almost 9,000 shivering fans chanting, "We're No. 1! We're No. 1!" Mixed with echoes of mountain man Yosef's thunderous long rifle blasts, the stadium rocked.

Fans nicknamed Kidd Brewer Stadium "The Rock" after their undefeated regular season. The Mountaineers had lost only once there since the 1993 disaster. Every team that came to The Rock knew they were in for a real battle, and very few had come away victorious.

On the sideline in front of the Mountaineers' bench, Scott Satterfield was walking around slapping the helmets of his teammates. "This is it. We gotta beat these guys. We've worked too hard to lose now. Our coaches have done all they can. It's up to us now. Damon, this is your night, man. Let's go out there and show them some Mountaineer football," he yelled to the receiving team as they trotted onto the field, accompanied by a roar from the electrified ASU side of The Rock.

Across the field there were a few hardy Texans bunched up behind the Lumberjacks' bench on the Stephen F. Austin side of the stadium. Their best effort to respond to the bouncing cheerleaders leading the raucous Mountaineer fans was drowned out.

Satterfield, the walk-on quarterback, and all those freshmen who were pressed into action in 1993 were seasoned veterans now, working together as a finely tuned machine. They had marched through twelve straight opponents, a grinding schedule of tough teams that reached down deep each week to try and derail the Mountaineers' perfect season. But each time the determined Apps found a way to preserve their unblemished record.

The accolades of Coach Moore's pregame press conference about his old friend Coach Pearce, however, were not coach-speak flattery. The No. 7–seeded Lumberjacks, who were 11-1, came to The Rock to win.

They were not intimidated by the high-scoring Mountaineer offense or stingy defense. They came out strong from the opening kickoff and let the Mountaineers know they were in the game of their lives. The strong running offense that was the Mountaineers' main weapon all season was held to a season low of 72 yards. All-conference tailback Damon Scott, who came into the game with an ASU single-season best of 1,452 yards, was smothered all night. He only gained 16 yards on 12 carries.

Satterfield, a senior now, carried the load for Appalachian. He completed 21 of 33 passes for 200 yards and two touchdowns and led the team in rushing with 43 yards on 15 carries. But it wasn't enough.

Even though they were manhandled on both sides of the scrimmage line, the Mountaineers managed to carry a 17-13 lead late into the final quarter.

The Lumberjacks weren't in the mood to concede defeat. With the game clock showing 6:40, SFA was deep in its own territory. Quarterback James Ritchey drove his team, with tailback Leonard Harris relentlessly grinding out long chunks of yardage, until they reached midfield. Ritchey then shocked everyone with a gutsy call in defiance of his coach's sideline instructions.

"Coach said to run the ball no matter what defense Appalachian was showing us. We had a run called, but when they brought their two safeties up and had nine men on line, I called an audible for a streak pattern for Jefferson," Ritchey told reporters after the game.

The pass was a 49-yard touchdown reception by Chris Patterson who ran untouched into the Mountaineer end zone. The Lumberjacks tacked on another score for insurance in their 27-17 win. It was a bitter end to an almost perfect season for the Mountaineers.

The glow from 1995's perfect pre-play-off record lost some of its shine on opening day the next September. The Wake Forest Demon Deacons hung a 19-13 loss on the Mountaineers. Appalachian regrouped and won the next three in a row and finished out the 1996 season at 7-4. Not bad, but not good enough to get into the play-offs. The loss to Furman kept them out of the conference championship and denied them an automatic play-off bid.

Even though they were ignored in the play-offs, the Mountaineers still clung to some bragging rights by keeping the Old Mountain Jug for the eighth straight year with a 24-17 win over Western Carolina in Cullowhee. It was little consolation for not being in the play-offs, but it was a matter of pride that the jug hadn't left Boone since Jerry Moore had been head coach. The following year ASU posted an identical record with no invitation to the play-offs. It seemed that the Mountaineers were in a 7-4 rut.

⋄

The 1998 Mountaineers reeled off five straight wins including an impressive 26-13 win over the Furman Paladins at The Rock. The Furman games developed a pattern in which the home team always won.

High Country fans were getting a little disgruntled at the two-year play-off drought. But as he always seemed to do when dissension mounted, Moore coached his 1998 team to the play-offs again. They beat Tennessee State in a wild free-scoring game, treating the Boone faithful to a 45-31 romp in the first round. The big victory was an outlet for frustration after a humiliating 23-6 upset loss in Cullowhee at the hands of Western Carolina the week before. They had to leave the Old Mountain Jug there for the first time in 10 years.

Louisiana hospitality abounded when Appalachian arrived in Natchitoches for their return to the play-off series. Sadly it only lasted until the whistle sounded for the opening kickoff. Northwestern State raced to a 31-20 win over the punchless Mountaineers.

The fierce rivalry with Furman didn't look so fierce at Greenville in 1999. The Paladins laid a 35-21 whipping on the Mountaineers and forced them to share the Southern Conference co-championship with Furman and Georgia Southern. Winning the championship is the Mountaineers' goal every season and sharing it was good enough to get them into the play-offs again. They closed out the 20th century with two consecutive play-off appearances but were unable to advance beyond the quarterfinals. Some consolation, however, was found when they reclaimed the Old Mountain Jug with a 34-10 trouncing of Western Carolina at The Rock.

Jerry: *We don't talk a lot about national championships and rankings during the season. Our goal is to win the Southern Conference Championship for an automatic bid to the play-offs. We work hard every day at practice to be ready to play our opponent that week, whether it's LSU, Michigan, Furman, or Georgia Southern. It doesn't matter who our opponent is, we walk onto that field with the attitude that we can win that game. We don't always win, but you have to believe that you can.*

It all goes back to my high school coach, M. B. Nelson. He taught us to have that winning spirit. My coaches and I try to instill that same spirit in our players. It's not realistic to think you're going to win every game, but I promise you, if a team walks onto the field thinking they are going to lose, I guarantee you they will.

Football games are won and lost in a lot of different ways. There are mistakes, bad breaks, any number of things that can happen in the game to affect the outcome. But if a team plays to the best of its ability and still loses, I'm just as proud of them.

THE FURMAN RIVALRY—
MOUNTAINEER MAGIC

Jerry: *There was a lot of hype about the new millennium with 2000 being a new beginning, but I don't pay a lot of attention to that stuff. We practiced and played the same way we did in the last century. Nothing changed. We worked hard at practice and the big game was always the one coming up on Saturday.*

Our rivalry with Furman goes back a long way and is one of the biggest in the league. They've had a long tradition of winning big games, and we have built up a pretty good reputation as a winner ourselves.

We knew we were in for some tough games in the early days of that 2000-2004 series. Both teams had strong defenses that held the score down. But they had the nation's top runner in Louis Ivory back then; the new century didn't change that. They beat us pretty bad down there in '99, but our defense got together before the 2000 game and said they would stop Ivory and give our offense the chance to score.

Those early 2000 games were some of the most exciting games played anywhere, with most of the final scores not decided until the last minute of the game. It really gave fans a treat.

2000—The Rock

The 21st century brought new intensity, if that was possible, to Appalachian's longstanding rivalry with Furman. Beginning with the 2000 game in Boone, the stage was set for a five-game series that some described as the most exciting or most miraculous, contests ever played in college football.

From the 2000 through the 2004 seasons the average winning margin by either team was two points. And The Rock lived up to its reputation as being a tough place for visitors to win. Appalachian won four of the five games, including one at the Paladins' home field.

As predicted by area sportswriters, the 2000 game was a slugfest in the trenches. Except for two long plays, Furman's offense was held in check. Those two long plays, however, gave the Paladins a 14-3 lead at halftime.

Mountaineer defensive end Jimmy Freeman said, "Our offense was moving the ball the first half, but we just weren't getting the ball into the end zone. Except for a couple of big plays, we pretty much stopped them. Once we got in sync and stopped them from making big plays, I knew we would get it into the end zone eventually because we've got a lot of talent over there."

The ASU offense, with first-time starter Joe Burchette at quarterback, came to life in the second half. He picked the Paladins' defense apart with his passing arm. Burchette's successful aerial attack opened up the running game that had been held to a school-history low of 10 yards in the first half. The Mountaineers marched 53 yards in 10 plays in the third quarter down to the Paladins' one-yard line. With the nose of the ball touching the hash mark, Burchette sneaked it over for the Mountaineers' first touchdown.

"Time out," Coach Moore yelled to the referee standing a few yards away on the edge of the playing field. Burchette trotted over to the sidelines. "They will be expecting a run. We have to throw for two," Moore said as offensive coordinator Scott Satterfield gave Burchette the play.

Breaking from the huddle, the Mountaineers lined up in their usual Power-I-formation. The fans packed in Kidd Brewer Stadium rose to their feet in unison and shouted encouragement.

"Burchette checks the Paladin defense. Hands under center for the snap," lovable redheaded WKBC radio veteran announcer David Jackson said into his mike. "Everyone is on the line except for the two safeties," he continued in rapid fire with his voice rising. "The defense is jamming the middle, expecting a run. It's a short-snap count. Burchette has caught the defense by surprise. He pulls out, fakes a handoff to Beard plunging into the line. Burchette hides the ball on his hip and rolls to his right. Looks like he might run it. He pulls up short and throws a bullet to Wilcox all alone in the end zone! It's a new game, 14-11." The two-point conversion brought the Mountaineers to within a field goal to tie.

In the fourth quarter, a relieved Mountaineer crowd cheered the defense that played true to its promise and denied the Paladins a touchdown inside the 20-yard line. Furman had to settle for a field goal. The ASU student section came alive; the Mountaineers were still only a touchdown away at 17-11.

Burchette again methodically moved the Mountaineers 80 yards to the Paladins' two-yard line. The stage was set for another of those cardiac finishes Furman and Appalachian fans had become accustomed to. This time Burchette gave the handoff to Jerry Beard, who plowed into the end zone behind his offensive line to tie the score at 17-17. The Paladins called timeout to try to rattle Mountaineer kicker Mark Wright. More than 13,000 screaming fans were now on their feet, hoping for a miracle. The miracle was that the team could hear the signals being called.

After a second timeout, The Rock watched in stone silence as Wright calmly stepped up and split the uprights for the 18-17 win. The Mountaineers had done it again!

The cold rarified mountain air suddenly exploded with a chorus of cheers led by cheerleaders and mascot Yosef running up and down the sideline firing his musket. Mountaineer fans shook The Rock for more than twenty minutes after the game to savor another miraculous win by Appalachian against their archrival Furman.

Down on the field, a reporter pushed his way through the ecstatic mob of players and fans surrounding Coach Moore. Working his way between two large black-and-gold uniformed bodies to get his recorder in front of the coach, reporter Steve Behr asked, "Coach, what do you think of your new quarterback Joe Burchette?"

In a deliberately understated response, Moore said, "I thought he did well. When our running game was shut down, he picked the offense up with almost 300 yards passing. On that last drive . . . he's probably going to be a guy his whole career who will throw the ball through some guy's hands because of the velocity he gets on the ball. Not a lot of guys could have gotten that ball between two defenders to Joey Gibson the way he did. Our defense delivered on their promise to stop Ivory; he was over 50 yards short of his game average."

The Mountaineers advanced to the Division I-AA semifinal play-off game and lost a heartbreaker to a good Montana team by a field goal, 19-16.

2001—Greenville, South Carolina

In the decades-long Furman-ASU rivalry, it always seemed the home team won. The 2001 meeting was no different. Furman came into the game ranked No. 3 nationally and Appalachian was No. 5. The teams were pretty evenly matched with 2-0 records and were tied for first place in the Southern Conference. The difference that could tip the scale was Louis Ivory, the previous year's Walter Payton Award–winner as Division I-AA player of the year.

As the players awaited the opening kickoff there was enough electricity in the air to generate a storm. All the tough talk was finished; it was time to put leather on leather. A thundering cheer filled the air after the final note of the national anthem sounded. The referee's whistle shrilled as he dropped his arm to signal the kickoff. The battle was on. Brian Bratton stunned the Mountaineers to the delight of a packed Paladin stadium with a 100-yard touchdown return on the opening kickoff. Furman had a seven-point lead with only 16 clicks off the game clock.

The game settled into a sluggish contest with neither line giving up much running room. Mountaineer tailback Jerry Beard ripped off a 13-yard touchdown run to start the second quarter and even up the score at seven apiece. It didn't last long. Ivory responded with an 18-yard touchdown run, breaking tackles on his charge into the end zone for a 14-7 lead at halftime.

The second half didn't go much better for the Mountaineers' offense, which couldn't get on track the first half. Billy Napier's long touchdown passes of 30 and 39 yards to wide receiver Isaac West caught the stubborn Appalachian defense by surprise. The air strikes built a 28-14 lead late in the second half of the game.

Poor field position, costly mistakes, and penalties kept the Mountaineers' offense bottled up most of the afternoon. They had difficulty running and passing against the strong Paladin defense but managed one final score with 1:56 left in the game. The 28-22 final score silenced the Appalachian fans. The Mountaineers were supposed to win these games with a last-minute miracle. This time, however, they were fresh out of miracles.

"We're not a team that thrives on big plays. We're a team that thrives on driving the ball and sustaining ball control, and we couldn't do that," Moore said in a voice that echoed his despair to reporters gathered outside the locker room. "I was disappointed in the 11 penalties, most on the offense. Poor punts led to good field position and points for them. I was especially disappointed in the unsportsmanlike-conduct penalty.

"I thought in the fourth quarter when we had the wind, we'd be in good shape," Moore said, "but we punted the ball 20 yards with the wind. You just don't do that and win.

"They did nothing new," Moore said of the long touchdown strikes. "The two post routes are the same ones they ran against Wyoming last week.

"I don't want to take one thing away from Furman because they played very well. But we're the ones that caused the long yardage with 15-yard penalties, the holding penalties, the unsportsmanlike call. Stuff like that really hurt us," Moore concluded.

While the offense took the heat for their inconsistent play, there was praise for the defensive line. They held Louis Ivory to only 40 yards rushing. Appalachian's four down linemen were in his face all day, particularly tackles John Marino and Ryan Watson.

The incentive for the outstanding defensive-line play came courtesy of the *Greenville News* in Friday's edition. An article passed around the Mountaineers' dressing room prior to the game contained a quote from Ivory. When asked if he thought he could make the 50 yards he needed to become Furman's all-time rushing leader in the upcoming game, Ivory replied, "I feel like I can gain 100 yards against them; 50 more than the necessary 50 yards I need." The Mountaineers' response denied Ivory his boast for at least another week.

Despite their disappointing loss to Furman, Appalachian still made the play-offs with eight conference wins. They advanced to the quarterfinals before their old nemesis, Georgia Southern, sent the Mountaineers home with a 38-24 loss.

2002—Mountaineer Miracle

> Jerry: *Furman has always been tough for us. We have been fortunate the last several years to have won some close games that could have gone either way. Our players did some good things responding to tough situations, especially that 2002 game they called the Mountaineer Miracle. I'll be honest, I thought it was over and was ready to congratulate our guys. They played one heck of a game . . . win or lose.*

If the 13,000-plus Appalachian fans who witnessed the 18-17 last-second win in 2000 thought that was a miracle finish, they would never forget October 11, 2002.

It was a chilly autumn afternoon at The Rock. The temperature started dropping as soon as the sun sank behind the mountains. As often happened, the game would determine if the Mountaineers, nationally ranked No. 4, would win the Southern Conference Championship by beating Furman, who was ranked No. 5 in national polls. Both teams were primed for battle. The ASU warriors lined up, snorting and digging their cleats into the artificial turf like bulls ready to charge the purple-clad Paladins.

The Mountaineers and Paladins battled back and forth the first half; both defenses grudgingly yielded little yardage to the powerful running offenses. Only a field goal by Furman showed on the scoreboard at the half.

With his team trailing 6-0 after the Paladins' second field goal, Jay Lyles picked off a pass by the Southern Conference's leading passer, Billy Napier, and returned it untouched for a Mountaineer go-ahead touchdown, 7-6. Kicker Danny Marshall kept Furman in the game with his third field goal to give the Paladins a slim 9-7 lead.

Appalachian answered with a 54-yard drive to Furman's 24-yard line. A Joe Burchette pass found Joey Hoover all alone 15 yards from the nearest defender for an easy 24-yard touchdown to take a 14-9 lead.

"I thought we were just going to run down the clock and kick the field goal," Burchette said. "But coach sent in a pass play. It was a great call and Joey ran a great route. I had seen the play run on TV and showed it to the coaches and we put it in."

The Paladins weren't through yet. They roared back, driving 73 yards, which consumed 5:32 of clock time. A 12-yard pass to Bear Rinehart crossing the middle of the end zone with only 7.4 seconds remaining gave the Paladins a 15-14 lead. A jubilant Furman team thought they had it won. Shocked Appalachian fans were faced with the possibility that Furman had come to The Rock and fought their way to a narrow upset. They couldn't possibly pull this one out. Where were those last-second heroics their ardent fans were so accustomed to seeing the Mountaineers pull off?

All that was left was for Furman to kick the extra point and nail the Mountaineers' coffin shut. A despondent crowd watched as the Paladins huddled back on the 10-yard line, waiting for Marshall to come out and seal the win with a routine conversion kick.

"There seems to be some discussion among Furman's coaches on the sidelines," announcer David Jackson said. "Marshall, Furman's kicker, steps onto the field. No, check that. He's called back by Coach Bobby Lamb and Napier is trotting back on the field. This is unbelievable! The Paladins are going for two!" Jackson exclaimed.

"The Paladins come to the line of scrimmage, linemen pointing at the Mountaineers' front four dug in, poised for the snap. The backs are in close, expecting a pass from Napier who is 20 of 29 on the night.

"Napier checks the defense. He's bobbing right and left, barking out the signal. He takes the snap, pulls out from under center, and drops back deep. He's being chased by John Mannino but fires a screen pass before being buried by Mannino and K. T. Stovall.

"It's intercepted! Josh Jefferies intercepts Napier's pass intended for running back Torieco O'Neal on the 18-yard line. He takes a few steps . . . He laterals to Black!" Jackson shouted into the mike. "It's a footrace now with Napier and running back O'Neal in hot pursuit. They are the only two men between Black and the end zone 82 yards away! They are swept away by Jefferies and a host of Mountaineer blockers.

"Black crosses the goal line! Two points for the Black and Gold! This is unbelievable! Appalachian has won an incredible 16-15 victory on the two-point conversion interception! It's a Mountaineer miracle!"

The standing-room-only Appalachian fans celebrated uncontrollably in the stands and poured down onto the field. They couldn't believe what they had seen. Just seconds earlier they were resigned to an upset at the hands of archrival Furman. Jubilant Mountaineer players hoisted Black up on their shoulders and carried him off the field shouting, "Can you believe it?"

But hold everything. The clock didn't start because of the two-point conversion attempt and there were still seven seconds left in the ball game. Appalachian was penalized for excessive celebration, and Furman lined up on the 45-yard line for the kickoff.

Marshall topped the onside kick right to, who else, Josh Jefferies, the big defensive end who made the game-winning interception. Jefferies downed the ball to preserve an incredible win.

Reporters rushed down onto the field and tried to interview the celebrating Mountaineer team, who were still jumping up and down, hugging and back-slapping the two men of the hour—Josh Jefferies and Derrick Black.

"What just happened out there?" Steve Behr of the *Watauga Democrat* shouted at Black, trying to overcome the loud celebration going on around them.

"They had been doing the out pattern the whole game," Black said. "Jay picked one off in the third quarter. So I had been playing soft on it like Coach wanted to play it, but we played a different technique on it this time. And Josh always said that if he got a pick or a fumble, he was going to pitch it back to me. And he did. He pitched it, and I did the rest."

Furman players walked off the field in a daze, picking their way through the celebrating Mountaineer players and the fans who had flooded the field to congratulate their team.

"I thought we did it," leading Furman receiver and touchdown maker Bear Rinehart said, still in shock. "I thought we were going to be the winner in tomorrow's paper. I sure thought it was in the bag."

"The call got mixed up," Coach Lamb said in the somber Furman dressing room. "It was supposed to be a sprint out, and we ended up throwing a screen pass. Lamb was still shaking his head in disbelief. "I've lost a lot of games, but I've never lost one like today. I take full responsibility for it," he said. "We'll evaluate and see what we've got to do next time."

The irony of this win was lurking in the memories of some of the alumni dancing and cheering down on the field of victory. The '02 game was Coach Bobby Lamb's first visit back to The Rock since he quarterbacked the Paladins in a 21-14 losing effort on that same field. As he walked off the field, students dragged the goalposts past him, just like they did in 1984 as he trudged dejectedly off the field.

In the Mountaineers' dressing room, the players were still whooping and hollering and high-fiving each other on their miraculous comeback.

Coach Moore shook hands and hugged excited players still in their uniforms. A big smile covered his face when he stated the obvious to waiting reporters: "He knows how to score," he said, referring to Black. "He's probably our leading scorer. He's already returned a blocked field goal and a fumble for touchdowns this year. And tonight he made a miracle in returning that lateral from Jefferies for 82 yards. It was just awesome.

"Furman scored with seven seconds left. Most people would have just gone through the motions on the two-point conversion," a jubilant Coach Moore said, "but not Josh Jefferies and not our defense!

"Was I upset about the penalty for celebrating? Not at all." Coach Moore smiled. "If you can't celebrate after doing what we did today, then there's something wrong with college sports."

Defensive coach John Wiley was even more elated. "It was an emotional ending because we had played them well all day long. Then they stuck that last pass in for a touchdown and we were immediately deflated, even to the point that I just put in a basic call on that last play out of frustration. There was no thought put into the call at all; just line up and play. Then Josh picked off the tunnel screen and all of a sudden he was running down the sideline. I saw the ball pitched back to Black, and the excitement started to build, and all of a sudden he scored."

Wiley was standing beside Coach Moore when Black scored. He said, "You know what, they still have to kick off to us, don't they?"

Coach Moore answered, "Yeah . . . they do."

"Well, Coach, we just won this ball game," Wiley said, laughing out loud and clapping his hands as the defense came running off the field carrying Black. "Good job, guys, that was fantastic."

Jerry: *After it turned out the way it did, I called Bobby [Lamb] Sunday morning. He's one of my best friends, and I just wanted to talk to him and his wife, Allyson. I related some experiences I'd had while coaching and just wanted him to have a little peace of mind about that play. But I never, ever asked him why they called that play.*

"Mountaineer Miracle" was the large, extra-bold headline on the sports page of the *Watauga Democrat*. Just below the headline was a photograph of Derrick Black being carried off the field by his teammates.

Unknown to Coach Moore, All-American defensive end Josh Jefferies and cornerback Black had made a pact three weeks before the game. They agreed that if Jefferies ever made an interception he would pitch it pack to Black. They could not possibly have known what an impact their agreement would make on the game and their season.

The win knocked the Paladins out of contention for the conference championship. There were no Mountaineer miracles in their first-round play-off game, however. The Bears of Maine pulled a switch and had their own miracle game. Appalachian blew a 10-point lead and was edged out by a late fourth-quarter score, giving the Bears a come-from-behind 14-13 win.

2003—Upset in Greenville

Jerry: *Every year we play Furman it's a dogfight. That year [2003] wasn't any different. The outcome usually determined if we went to the play-offs or not. We were both ranked, and we faced two tough teams in Georgia Southern and No. 1–ranked Wofford after that. Wofford beat us and won the conference championship undefeated. They advanced to the semifinals and we stayed home.*

The Mountaineers headed south to Greenville for their annual war with Furman. To this point, the three contests of the new century had been bruising, low-scoring contests. The only bankable odds seemed to be the home-field advantage. That is until the Furman public-address announcer, in his pregame analysis said, "The Appalachian defensive line, namely the tackles, are soft and are the weakness of the defensive line."

Fired up by the put-down from Furman's announcer, Mountaineer defensive end K. T. Stovall led an inspired Mountaineers defense that stuffed the Paladin offense all night. Stovall collected three sacks and forced a fumble, which he recovered.

Appalachian scored first on a field goal, but Furman answered with a touchdown. Four minutes before the half, the Mountaineers drove 80 yards in 10 plays to score the go-ahead touchdown for a 10-7 halftime lead. A third-quarter field goal edged the Mountaineers to a 6-point lead.

Defenses for both teams stiffened and the best either offense could do was kick field goals. Furman's Coach Lamb opted for a sure three points from the 9-yard line late in the final quarter. He didn't want to risk his backup quarterback, Josh Stepp, who was subbing for injured starter Moore, turning the ball over on fourth down. He felt there was time to come back for another score. Furman fans didn't agree and unleashed a thundering roar of boos in protest.

With the Mountaineers leading 13-10 and 2:40 left on the clock, Furman held the Mountaineers on downs. The Paladins received the punt and moved it down to the Mountaineers' 45-yard line with 2:07 showing on the scoreboard clock. Coach Lamb again felt that was plenty of time for his team to score and win the game.

The Mountaineer defense had other ideas. They kept the Paladins out of field-goal range, and this time the Paladins went for it on fourth and long. Stepp was sacked by Stovall for an 8-yard loss, and fumbled the ball out of bounds. The jubilant defense came off the field to the applause of grateful fans. Richie Williams took a knee and the Mountaineers took home another nerve-racking win over Furman.

Once again the defense had bailed out the underperforming offense to preserve the 13-10 win. It was the first time since 1995 the Mountaineers had beaten the Paladins on their home field.

2004—Another Mountaineer Miracle

The bleachers at Kidd Brewer Stadium shook under the stomping feet of a near sellout crowd of 15,311 students and High Country fans. The Mountaineers and Paladins didn't disappoint them. Richie

Williams broke two NCAA records when he completed 28 straight passes and finished the night hitting 40 of 45 passes. But it wasn't his passing that had the final say.

"Furman quarterback Ingle Martin has his team on their own 48-yard line with only 1:25 left on the clock, trailing 23-21," said broadcaster David Jackson. "Martin drops back and rifles a screen pass to Cedric Gibson. He's got room and blockers in front of him. He may go all the way! He's to the 40, 30, 20, 10, he scores! Cedric Gibson breaks a screen pass into a 52-yard scoring dash to go ahead of the Mountaineers with just over a minute left in the game! Appalachian fans are on their feet. Furman lines up and fullback Mays punches it in for two points and a 29-23 lead."

Appalachian took the kickoff and moved to the Paladins' 13-yard line riding the arm of Richie Williams. With 35 seconds remaining on the game clock, both sides of Kidd Brewer Stadium rose screaming.

"The Mountaineers set up on the 13-yard line without a huddle. Williams is standing alone facing the sideline. The play is signaled in, he turns and barks signals with only 35 seconds left in the game. Five receivers spread out against Furman's prevent defense. The snap. Richie cocks his arm to pass. It's a fake. He brings it down, runs it up the gut, and scores untouched! Unbelievable! Appalachian wins 30-29! Wow! It's the third year in a row the Mountaineers have come from behind in the last minute of the game to beat Furman."

A reporter shouted over the noisy commotion of a celebrating team and thousands of happy fans, "Coach, how do you keep doing it to Furman with these last-minute comebacks?"

"It was just one of those great college football games," he said. "I told our players in pregame, there are a lot of big games in the country. You had Oklahoma and Texas fixing to kick off about an hour after we ate. You had the USC and Cal game, but I'll tell you the best game in college football today is going to take place in our stadium." Moore proved he wasn't only a wizard as a coach but a prophet as well.

Jerry: *We managed to beat Furman in some really great college football games. If the fans thought we deliberately waited until the last minute to score and win, believe me, we didn't. Those were hard-fought games. Because our players never gave up we were able to win those close games.*

RUMBLING AT THE ROCK— WINNERS BUT NOT CHAMPIONS

Jerry: *There were a lot of distractions in 2004. Our athletic director resigned and a new chancellor was brought in. I tried not to let it bother our football team and stayed out of it.*

I knew we had to do something to shake things up on our team. There were some discipline problems to take care of to get our team back on track. There was just a lot of stuff going on that we had to deal with.

I knew we had to change our offense. We had gone as far as we could go with the Power-I and to take advantage of our speed, I wanted to try a no-huddle spread formation. I had studied teams like West Virginia, Bowling Green, and Utah, who were using that offense very effectively. When we arrived in West Virginia, Coach Rich Rodriguez was really great. He gave our coaches full run of the place and talked to them at length about the no-huddle spread offense. We were pretty excited when we came back.

We decided to try using it in spring practice. The players liked it as well as we did. We really weren't going to go full-time into the spread offense like we've ended up doing. We were going to use it to start the game or second half or maybe after a nice punt return—just a little wrinkle to change up the tempo of the game. We needed something new to give us a little edge. That was what we started out to do, but we liked it so well, we haven't huddled since.

We had a lot of injuries to some of our key defensive players that season who didn't come back until the last two or three games. Our offense scored a lot of points to keep us from having a losing season. That Chattanooga game was like a track meet; I couldn't believe we scored 56 points and still lost.

The new no-huddle offense, installed in the beginning of the 2004 season, revved up Appalachian's offensive scoring average. Abandoning the Power-I running formation of 15 years for the spread, with only the quarterback in the backfield, saw the pass take center stage on offense. To help balance their attack, a running back would sometimes line up off the right or left side of the quarterback to allow option plays.

The first game with the new no-huddle spread offense didn't go well at all. Coach Moore was almost ready to drop the spread formation after the 53-7 whipping Wyoming gave the Mountaineers.

On the flight back to Boone, Coach Moore said to his coaches, "It was terrible; we looked awful. We would have done better staying in the Power-I. At least we would've known what we were doing."

Appalachian's offense got better as the season progressed, but the defense gave up too many points. The Mountaineers were fortunate to salvage a winning season at 6-5, but had no chance to make the play-offs for the second time in two years.

The Mountaineers hadn't gone two consecutive years out of the play-offs since the 1996 and 1997 seasons. Some alumni and fans were unhappy and expressed their feelings to the Appalachian coaches and administration as well.

High Country fans wanted their team to win a national championship, and to do that they had to get back into the play-offs. They had a potential championship team in the undefeated 1995 team but got tripped up in the quarterfinals. In 2000, a field goal kept them from advancing to the championship game. After that, the Mountaineers began to gradually slide downhill. Confidence that Jerry Moore could take them to a championship was beginning to slip.

What the fans didn't see that Jerry Moore saw was a young team that was evolving with a new spread offense that could score a lot of points fast. The job at hand was to shore up the defense, and they would have a formidable team to be reckoned with in 2005.

The difference in the way coaches see things and the way fans see them is fans want instant gratification by winning every week. Coaches are always building for the future. The future becomes the present when good players recruited each year can sustain a winning program. With few seniors, Moore and his staff saw promise for the next two years. None of that mattered to the disappointed alumni and High Country fans. They were accustomed to better from Coach Moore and many felt it was time for him to go.

The Mountaineers' new high-flying offense managed to squeeze by in 2004 with a 6-5 season, while averaging 34 points a game. The record didn't bother Coach Moore. He knew changing the offense was a risk, but it was a risk he felt had to be taken to advance the Mountaineers to the next level—a national championship. The decision to change wasn't made lightly. He and his staff had spent countless hours studying game films of successful spread-offense programs. Those programs used the spread-offense system to average more than 35 points a game. Coach Moore knew that offense would get the Mountaineers to the championship. He knew the 2004 team wasn't there yet, but they weren't far away, just like at Texas Tech when he was fired.

Unhappy fans and alumni lit up message boards calling for Jerry Moore's job. Some messages said, at age 65, Moore didn't have it anymore; he was getting too old and should retire. One complained loudly that he didn't recruit well. Others just called for a change.

There was pressure put on the athletic department, but with all the turmoil going on in the university's top administration, it simmered on the back burner. In the fans' minds, either Coach Moore or athletic director Roachel Laney had to go; some wished to replace both.

Rumors flew all over campus. One said that Coach Moore was called to the chancellor's office and told to let his son Chris go, along with some other coaches. Reportedly Coach Moore wouldn't stand for that and said he'd quit first. That rumor proved to be false, but it was hard to tell fact from fiction for a while.

During the winter of 2004 and spring of 2005 there were some major changes in the university administration and in the athletic department. Dr. Kenneth Peacock became the new chancellor and Charlie

Cobb was hired as athletic director. They breathed new energy into the athletic program and set about solving problems and planning expansion and improvement of all the athletic facilities.

Immediately after the disappointing 2004 season-ending game loss to Western Carolina that drove the last nail into the Mountaineers' hopes for a play-off bid, Coach Moore immersed himself in solving the problems of his football team. He left the administrative upheaval for others to deal with. He gathered a group of about 20 players and team leaders. Closed-door meetings were held. He challenged them with questions like: What is it going to take to fix things and what are we doing that isn't working?

He had the players make a list of things they thought should be changed. The list included things like complaints of too much time standing around during practice; requests for a uniform dress code for road games; a desire for more discipline and more pride in themselves; as well as requests to paint the players' locker room and install new carpet on the floor.

Coach Moore took their suggestions and pared them down to a manageable list of doable changes. The response of the players prompted Moore to re-evaluate himself as a coach and mentor after more than 40 years in coaching. If he needed to change anything to make his team better, then he would make those changes.

Coach Moore had made a practice all his coaching life of studying other programs, always looking for ways to help his team be better. Just like he did when he changed the offense, he drove to Charlottesville, Virginia, in the spring of 2005. A meeting with Al Groh, head football coach of the University of Virginia Cavaliers, was arranged. Jerry watched them practice and studied their quick-paced timed drills, with players constantly moving from one drill station to the next. That looked like what his players wanted.

He came back and revamped the Mountaineer practice schedules so they more closely resembled a three-ring circus. Practice drills were changed to be run in timed segments, moving from one drill to the next with no dead time between. The players liked the new practice scheme and claimed the tempo made the game seem slow.

Jerry: *We were a young team that year* [2004] *but had some really good players. With Richie at quarterback, we knew we had made the right move with the new offense. We were sold on it from the start, but more important than that, the players bought into it. Changes in our practice routines also helped the players' attitude and work ethic; they really practiced hard.*

We knew there were some fans unhappy after our 2004 season. We weren't happy with it either, but we felt like we fixed the problems from that season and had laid the foundation for the future of this program. And it turned out that we were right.

Athletic director Charlie Cobb came on board in July of 2005, which ironically was the last year of Coach Moore's contract. That was no secret since it had been broadcast all over the Internet on message boards. It was a topic of conversation all around the High Country.

The coincidence wasn't lost on Jerry and Margaret Moore. The scenario was too similar to that dreaded final season at Texas Tech when athletic director T. Jones was in his first year.

Margaret: *You better believe it crossed our minds. We both felt it was happening all over again. Jerry didn't read the papers or message boards, but he knew there was pressure to fire him. We prayed about it and were ready for whatever happened. We were okay with it if that's the way it was to be. We were prepared. We left it in God's hands, and Jerry went on coaching just like he always did and didn't worry about those other things. Charlie was such a good guy, Jerry said he would resign before putting Charlie on the hot seat to fire him. That's the way Jerry felt about it.*

The dark days of winter slipped fitfully into spring as the atmosphere at The Rock took on an air of calm. Chancellor Peacock and Charlie Cobb started sorting out and addressing problems within the athletic department. A $32 million plan to update and expand all the athletic facilities was soon on the drawing board.

Chancellor Peacock was a veteran of more than 20 years at Appalachian in various positions of responsibility while working his way up. He knew his way around and provided the new energy and steadying leadership needed for the changes ahead. Cobb was a newcomer brought in from North Carolina State where he was heavily involved in a highly successful program in the Atlantic Coast Conference.

Aware of the unsettled atmosphere after the 2004 season, Cobb focused on learning the culture and people at Appalachian so he could help make it better.

"I didn't know Jerry at all," Charlie said, "but I had heard a lot of good things about him from people I trusted. I had learned that one of the keys to being a successful athletic director was to make sure your football and basketball coaches are in your corner. It was important that Jerry and I had a good working relationship from the very beginning. I think we achieved that."

Being the new man on campus, Charlie didn't feel the pressure of discontented fans and alumni. He believed the majority of the High Country fans were in Jerry's corner. There were a few he called the vocal minority who made most of the noise. There seemed to be a new energy swirling inside Owens Field House with Dr. Peacock, Appalachian's biggest fan, leading the way.

"When Dr. Peacock offered me the job, I asked him straight out if Jerry Moore was going to be the head coach," remarked Charlie Cobb. "He sent the ball back to my court and asked for my recommendation. I said I thought we should keep Jerry and that he would probably be here for a long while. Fortunately Jerry has made me look pretty good on that prediction.

"There was never any pressure on me to fire Jerry. I felt totally comfortable with my decision after I had a brief conversation with him about his position. I said we needed to talk about the future."

" 'Charlie,' he said, 'you don't have to worry about me. If it isn't going to work and I see it isn't going to work, you don't have to come talk to me about it. I'll resign.'

"That was it, that's all that was said. He's an awesome guy, an old ball coach. He's most comfortable in sweats, watching film, evaluating talent, and breaking down an opponent. I think that's something some of the new guys forget. That's what makes you successful—not being the media darling or the fans' favorite. It's preparing your players and coaches, and that's what Jerry Moore has done really well.

"His coaches tell me one of the greatest strengths Jerry has is evaluating talent in terms of being able to look at a kid that played running back in high school, but Jerry sees him as a defensive end. Or take a kid that played quarterback and turn him into a great receiver. He just has a tremendous talent to judge a kid's ability.

"Another big part of the success of this program is the number of walk-ons that come here, like All-Conference and All-American Kevin Richardson. He has broken nearly every school rushing and scoring record in the books. They get two or three really good ones every year because kids know Jerry will give them a chance. Look at our championship teams. In addition to Richardson, there's Nic Cardwell, Chase Laws, and Brad Coley. Richardson and Cardwell both scored touchdowns in the big win over Richmond. I couldn't be happier with our program and coaching situation here at ASU."

National Champions—
King of the Mountain

Jerry: *We had a really tough schedule in '05, no doubt about it. We looked at playing Kansas and LSU as an opportunity to see how good we were. We felt we could play with those guys. We didn't change our preparation for them except the coaches looked at some tapes of their games before the season started.*

We couldn't spend too much time on them. We had a tough conference schedule to think about. Those two games were a good deal for us. We got a lot of publicity and a nice paycheck. But the games didn't count toward the conference championship, and that's what we work for every year. The conference championship gave us an automatic play-off bid and we got to play at home. Playing teams at home makes a big difference. Not having to travel and playing for our students and hometown fans gave us a tremendous boost.

Looking at Appalachian's 2005 schedule, even the most ardent supporters could only groan at the sight of Kansas and LSU on the list. The Division I teams were bookends for Appalachian's tough traditional rivals—The Citadel, Furman, and Georgia Southern. There was no relief in the Mountaineers' schedule to look forward to.

Restless fans and alumni who were calling for Coach Moore's firing had been spoiled by Moore's legacy of having a winning season every year except one and going to the play-offs nearly every year since arriving at Appalachian in 1989. They had forgotten his courage in the face of their expressed doubts about his ability to win. And how he led the Mountaineers to a 9-3 record and to the play-offs his first season— a miraculous feat considering 52 members of the team left before he coached a single game. It was accomplished using a small core of remaining veterans and a host of untested freshmen and sophomores— a true testament to the caliber of the man Coach Jerry Moore was and the talent of his staff. His deep faith and confidence were strong; he was unflappable.

They had also forgotten how his team bounced back from its only losing season in 1993 with an undefeated season only two years later. Had they forgotten why Kidd Brewer earned the nickname The Rock? The last two seasons, the focus of their discontent, saw the Mountaineers go undefeated, winning all 11 games at home in 2003 and 2004. That was a convincing finish to an impressive 128 wins and only 34 losses in 16 seasons at The Rock.

The 2005 season started early in March at 6:30 A.M. in Varsity Gym. Those early morning workouts of multiple wind sprints, laps, and exercises to get the players in shape were grueling. There were trash cans with plastic liners conveniently placed around the gym floor to catch the athletes' breakfast without breaking stride in their workout.

> Jerry: *We had gotten away from our early morning workouts, but after our losing season in '93 we went back to them. Players and coaches rededicated themselves to football. It has been a good deal for us and has really paid off. The players didn't like it at first, but once they saw the results on the field they all look forward to it now. Most of the players come back each summer for strength-training camp; they are really a dedicated bunch of young men.*

After the early morning practice, Coach Moore paced back and forth in front of the huddled players who were trying to catch their breath. They listened intently to his motivational talk about teamwork, helping each other out, getting that winning spirit. Then he called on Kevin Richardson to talk to the players about helping each other on the field and what they needed to do to win a championship.

Even though their schedule included Kansas and LSU, Moore warned his players not to look ahead. The most important game of the season is the next game on the schedule, he has always told them. The message hasn't changed over the years.

Fans looked ahead to the two powerhouses, however. There wasn't a lot of optimism for the season and plenty of criticism for scheduling two tough Division I opponents. Sure, they were big money games, they said, but was it worth the humiliation?

> Jerry: *I've never had anything to do with scheduling games, that's somebody else's job. We just prepare the team the best we can. We don't work any harder for those big guys than we do for Furman or anybody else. We play every game to win. You have to believe you have a chance to win or you'll lose every time.*
>
> *It's always good to win that first game. That gets rid of the jitters for the new guys and lets the veterans establish their leadership roles. It was a confidence builder when your second game was with a top 10 team like Kansas.*
>
> *We took a pretty good beating out there, 36-8. But when I walked into the locker room after the game, those guys were dejected like we had lost a conference game. It wasn't one of those pick-up-the-check-and-come-home kind of deals. I knew right then that team had a chance to be special.*

After the big loss to Kansas, the team used that as a rallying point and expressed to each other their expectations to win the conference championship without actually saying it to Coach Moore. They put those expectations into practice, winning their next two games as warmups for Furman.

The Mountaineers had won the last three games against Furman, including one on the Paladins' home field. Now they were headed back to Greenville, South Carolina, for a must-win game, just like every year. The games were no longer the low-scoring defensive trench wars they used to be. The previous year's game had been a free-wheeling high-scoring affair won by the Mountaineers 30-29 in the last 30 seconds of the game. This year was expected to be no less exciting with two veteran quarterbacks in Ingle Martin for the Paladins and Richie Williams at the helm of the Mountaineers' attack.

Jerry: *The 2005 game had an added incentive for the Furman seniors; they had never beaten us. They were really primed for us to come down there and get it on. We won down there two years ago to break the homewinning cycle. We felt like we could do it again. It turned into one of those typical Furman-Appalachian ball games that were won in the last minute. It seemed like whoever had the ball last won the game.*

Appalachian and Furman butted heads in a passing duel between Williams and Martin. The Mountaineers won the battle of yardage 468-428 but lost the scoring war 34-31. Another miracle finish was in the making. The Paladins drove 74 yards in 15 plays late in the fourth quarter, eating 4:26 off the clock. Martin hit Patrick Sprague with a bullet pass from six yards out with 31 seconds left to take the lead.

There was apprehension among the Furman players, especially the seniors. It was too reminiscent of past Paladin drives in 2002 and 2004 when they took late-game leads against the Mountaineers only to lose in the last seconds. Could Richie Williams do it to them again?

Williams, who had rallied the Mountaineers with two fourth-quarter touchdowns, said, "I felt like we had a chance. We just had to go back out there and run our two-minute drill in 31 seconds."

Aided by Jermaine Little's 46-yard kickoff return, and the passing and running of Williams, Appalachian moved the ball down to Furman's 23-yard line with 3 seconds showing on the scoreboard clock. The standing-room-only crowd of more than 12,000 screaming fans became hysterical as the Mountaineers lined up to try a 41-yard field goal, well within Julian Rauch's range.

WKBC's David Jackson yelled into his mike, "Rauch steps off his kicking spot and calmly waits on the snap. The ball is down, Rauch gets the kick off, but it's tipped! It's tipped but is straight on course. It drops short in the end zone, and the Paladins hold off the Black and Gold for another cardiac finish, 34-31. Linebacker William Freeman broke through and got just enough of the ball to shorten its flight. What a disappointing finish for Richie Williams, who became only the second Mountaineer to generate 7,000 yards of career total offense," Jackson said. Then he signed off.

"I was glad for the seniors," Furman coach Bobby Lamb said. "It wasn't so much a monkey off my back, but a monkey off the backs of our seniors. They came close as freshmen, only to see Josh Jefferies and Derrick Black pull off the Mountaineer Miracle because of my bad decision, and they beat us with seven seconds left in the game. We had the lead again only to lose it in the last minute their sophomore year. And last year—well, what can I say—Richie Williams shredded us with his passing and beat us with his touchdown run with 30 seconds on the clock. I wasn't sure he wasn't going to do it to us again this year, but our guys reached down for that little extra and pulled this one out."

The Mountaineers regrouped and beat three tough conference opponents in Georgia Southern, Wofford, and Tennessee-Chattanooga before flying south to take on LSU.

Jerry: We flew in there and played our game and flew back that night after the game. There were a lot of displaced people in the area because of Hurricane Katrina. We didn't want to put anybody out by taking up hotel space. Appalachian State University students did something really special by presenting a check for $20,000 to the Louisiana State University Foundation Student Relief Fund during halftime at Tiger Stadium. The money was raised by different student groups on campus. The 91,000 LSU fans gave us a standing ovation. It was a pretty neat deal. We received hundreds of emails thanking ASU students for their generosity.

The game was a different story. We were only 14 points behind in the third quarter. Even when LSU had us down 24-0 in the last quarter they still had some of their first team in there. We had Western Carolina the next week for a crucial must-win game for the conference championship and home-field advantage in the play-offs.

I started pulling our first team guys out in the middle of the third quarter. They didn't pull theirs out until we did. I think we played well against the No. 2 team in the nation. We got a nice check, but that's not why we play the big schools. We believe it makes us a better team for it and helps our recruiting.

After suffering their first shutout in 13 years, the Mountaineers took out their frustrations on Western Carolina 35-7 the following week to reclaim the Old Mountain Jug after a year of turmoil at ASU. It was a different atmosphere on The Rock now for the Mountaineers.

They had roared through their conference schedule, except for Furman. Their new spread offense was running on all cylinders under Richie Williams' direction at quarterback. Appalachian's final tune-up before the play-offs was a 52-14 thrashing of Elon.

The Mountaineers disposed of Lafayette and Southern Illinois in the first two play-off rounds, adding 72 points to their season high of 333. No one actually said it out loud, but many felt divine intervention had given them another shot at archrival Furman in the semifinals to even the score.

Appalachian had the advantage of playing at home in a series that always favored the home team. Ingle Martin, however, had already led his Paladins to a come-from-behind win over the Mountaineers in their regular-season game. But this was the play-offs, a new season for both teams. All bets were off; the winner played for the championship the following week.

The Mountaineers gave the 15,000 black-and-gold faithful plenty to cheer about by taking an early lead on Kevin Richardson's 4-yard touchdown run to cap off a 70-yard opening drive. The Paladins were forced to punt their next possession. Appalachian started another methodical march with Richardson's slashing runs and Richie Williams' sharp passing. Richie worked the Mountaineers down to the Paladins' 45-yard line. The mood turned somber at The Rock when Williams got up limping after an 11-yard scamper.

"I thought I could walk on it, but I couldn't. That's when I called time out," said the injured Williams.

But the Mountaineers didn't miss a beat. Backup Trey Elder came in and threw a 45-yard touchdown pass to Dexter Jackson on his first play to increase the Mountaineers' lead to 14-0 with six minutes left to play in the opening period.

Richardson scored his second touchdown in the second quarter, but it was Appalachian's only score, while the Paladins took control of the game and put up 23 points to take a halftime lead of 23-21. Both defenses tightened up in the third quarter to stop drives inside each other's 10-yard line.

Elder led a sustained 76-yard Mountaineer drive midway through the fourth quarter that featured six straight runs by Richardson and pass completions to Dexter Jackson. Elder took it in himself for the go-ahead score that atoned for his previous fumble inside Furman's

10-yard line. Elder then hit William Mayfield in the end zone for a two-point conversion to take a 29-23 lead, with 4:30 showing on the clock.

The game looked like it was going to be another one of those wild last-minute finishes. Thick, cold December air hung like a fog at The Rock. Furman quarterback Ingle Martin drove the Paladins into Mountaineer territory with less than 40 seconds left to play.

Steam rose from the sweaty linemen who had been at war all night as they faced each other across the line of scrimmage. With a first-and-10 from Appalachian's 36-yard line, Jason Hunter came in from his defensive-end position, beat his block, and unloaded on Martin trying to pass. Big Omarr Byrom picked up the loose ball and set sail for the Furman goal line. Byrom ran out of gas and was brought down at the one-yard line.

Not scoring didn't matter to anyone, except the senior Byrom, who wanted to take it into the end zone for his first touchdown. The Mountaineers ran out the remaining 13 seconds with Williams taking a knee.

Students poured down onto the playing field and took down the goalposts to celebrate the Black and Gold's first trip to Chattanooga for a championship match-up against Northern Iowa.

Jerry: I thought it was awesome what those students did at the end. I thought I was going to get reprimanded for saying that, too. But that was just part of college football. That's one of the reasons why we do this. You can't take the fun out of it and I thought those students were awesome to come out like they did.

Championships are what we play for, why we worked so hard every practice during the season and off-season, too. I had been there in Chattanooga the past six or seven years, sitting in the bleachers, and every year I came back and thought, hey, we can play there. It was a long time coming. It's the big payoff and was really a big deal for us and the players. The news talked all week about whether Richie would start or not. We weren't worried. Trey came in the week before against Furman and played really well for us. We knew we could depend on Trey if Richie couldn't go. They were dedicated quarterbacks that laid it all out for their team and school.

2005 National Championship—Appalachian State vs. Northern Iowa

An excited crowd of more than 10,000 Appalachian fans followed the Black and Gold to Chattanooga for the cold mid-December game. Also in that crowd were close to 1,000 former Appalachian football players packing the stands on the Mountaineers' side.

It was a day that Appalachian State Coach Jerry Moore wondered if he would ever see: playing for the Division I-AA national championship. When he replaced Sparky Woods at Appalachian, expectations were high. That hadn't changed. Moore had coached the Mountaineers to the play-offs 11 times, but this was his first trip to the finals.

Changing the offense to the no-huddle spread was the answer he envisioned to advance the Mountaineers to the championship level. With that accomplished, all that was left to complete his dream was to enjoy the mini–Super Bowl atmosphere and beat Northern Iowa on Friday night.

The championship game was also a reward for the coaches' wives. They were the ones who dealt with their husbands' absences on recruiting trips and road games. Unlike most head coaches, though, Jerry sent his coaches home after practice. He wanted them to spend "Boone time" with their families. He eliminated as much time away from home for his coaches as possible. He learned years ago at Arkansas the importance of family time for a more satisfied coaching staff.

Jerry: *It was cold and we worked out in a snowstorm on that Monday in Boone. We decided to go on up to Chattanooga early and left after dinner Tuesday and got there about midnight. I wanted the team rested and focused on winning their first championship. We have sort of a ritual that we do before game day with the team. We always show the team some kind of inspirational movie. The night before the championship game we showed the movie* Miracle on Ice, *about the U.S. hockey team that beat Russia against all the odds in the 1980 Olympics. When we are down in the locker room everybody has their own way of preparing themselves mentally.*

A few minutes before the game, our tight end Nic Cardwell was in the locker room with his Bible open reading from II Samuel 22 to the players. It was David's song of praise when the Lord delivered him from the hands of all his enemies. It reads: "It is God who arms me with strength and makes my way perfect . . . He makes my feet like the feet of a deer; He enables me to stand on the heights. He trains my hands for battle . . . I pursued my enemies and crushed them."

The seven-minute pregame warning sounded about that time; it was time to go do battle. My last words to them were, "At some point in our lives, we all say, why? Then we turn our life, our family, our job, our circumstances over to God, and let him have room to work."

Margaret: *After hearing about Nic reading scriptures to his teammates in the dressing room, that completed my number-seven story. It started out back in January when our associate pastor challenged us to read the Bible through. In reading it I didn't realize the number seven was used as much as it was. It started me thinking about how often it showed up that year. When Jerry told me about Nic that night at the championship, it gave me the perfect ending.*

This is my number-seven story that I've told a million times since then: 1) the year 2005 when added is seven; 2) Richie Williams' number was seven; 3) that year Jerry had coached 43 years, that added up to seven; 4) we were only supposed to play four home games—we played seven; 5) our hotel room number at Chattanooga was 1006 which added up to seven; 6) we played on December 16, added up to seven; 7) the seven-minute warning buzzer in the dressing room sounded when Jerry found Nic reading the scripture.

That was a good bunch of kids. Nic, Corey Lynch, and Billy Riddle were spiritual leaders of the team and were instrumental in starting a Bible study among the players. They met once a week on their own to study the scriptures. I think that's pretty rare these days.

Early in the morning on game day, Coach Moore, Richie, and the athletic trainer went down to the stadium to see if Richie could run; he couldn't. He had to settle for just loosening up his throwing

Photograph by Paul Sherar and Matt Powell/c 2007 BGEA

Above, Tight end Nic Cardwell reads scripture to his
teammates before each game.

Photograph by Paul Sherar and Matt Powell/c 2007 BGEA

Coach Moore and the team kneel in prayer before every game.

arm to keep warm that night in pregame, just in case he was needed. In spite of the warm hospitality of Chattanooga, the temperature
dropped quickly to the upper 30s as the sun went down before game
time. The team went through a spirited pregame warmup to keep their
muscles loose and prevent injury during the game.

> Jerry: *We had two courageous quarterbacks and leaders on
> our team. We had already decided on Thursday to start Trey and
> only use Richie if we just had to. We made our decision based on
> whether or not Trey could run the ball. We ran a lot of option and
> ran a lot of counter stuff. But they stopped the inside zone play the
> first half, which a lot of our option came off of.*
>
> *If we were just going to run the zone and not get the op-
> tion off of it, then we went with the guy with the most experience.
> We knew Richie couldn't run or maneuver, which were his major
> strengths, but his passing was still sharp. When he walked onto
> that field he took charge and everybody stepped it up a notch to
> protect their quarterback.*

An electrically charged atmosphere enveloped the $28 million
Finley Stadium that has been the home of the Division I-AA championship series since it was built in 1997. The two nationally ranked
teams, with identical 11-3 records, were evenly matched by the odds-
makers until Williams was injured in the Furman game. Even after
Trey Elder came in and led the Mountaineers to two scoring drives
against Furman, Northern Iowa became a slight favorite.

With a national television audience and more than 10,000
charged-up Appalachian fans cheering in the stands, the Mountaineers
struggled in the first half. Turnovers only minutes apart gave the Panthers two field goals for an early lead. The usually tough Mountaineer
defense gave up 10 more points after another turnover in the second
quarter to go to the locker room trailing 16-7. The Mountaineers' only
bright spot was a sustained drive with Kevin Richardson's short slashing runs and Elder's passing. Richardson had been stymied most of the
game and finally got on track and found the end zone from the five for
Appalachian's only score of the half.

The last play of the first half was a surprise dose of encourage-

Photograph by Paul Sherar and Matt Powell/c 2007 BGEA

Led by Corey Lynch *(center, front row)* and Nic Cardwell, an average of 40 players attended a voluntary weekly Bible study.

ment to a Mountaineer crowd that hadn't had much to cheer about. The ball was just barely on the Panthers' side of the 50-yard line and there was only time for one more play. Coach Moore turned to Richie and all he said was, "Hail Mary."

Richie limped out onto the field and was greeted by a suddenly re-energized Mountaineer team. The pass was incomplete, but the shot of adrenalin it pumped into the offense couldn't be measured in yards. During halftime, Moore asked Williams if he was ready to go back in.

"I'll give it a go," Williams said.

Hobbled by his injury, Williams managed to shave Northern Iowa's lead to just two points with a 79-yard, 11-play drive. But the Panthers' defense had hunkered down and kept the Mountaineers out of their end zone early in the fourth quarter. The situation was pretty grim with virtually no running game and a crippled quarterback trying to make the passing game work.

Then it happened, the play that made all the ESPN highlight shows and was the talk of the sports media for days. Most Appalachian fans agreed it eclipsed the "Mountaineer Miracle" as the most important play in Appalachian history.

A little more than nine minutes were left in the fourth quarter and that seemed like an eternity to a tiring defense. The defense jogged onto the field after a three-and-out punt had the ball on Northern Iowa's 21-yard line. Linebacker Monte Smith, tackle Joe Suiter, and defensive end Marcus Murrell decided among themselves that something needed to be done.

In the huddle Suiter said to the rest of the defensive players, "We need a score." The defense high-fived each other and vowed to raise their game up a notch to help out the flagging offense.

The Mountaineer defense held for two downs. On a third down and long, Panthers quarterback Eric Sanders dropped back looking for his receivers to make a first down and keep the clock moving.

"Sanders is looking for an open receiver." Announcer David Jackson's voice rose with anticipation. "Marcus Murrell comes from Sanders' blind side. Marcus knocks the ball out of Sanders' hand! The ball is on the ground! Jason Hunter picks it up! He's to the 10, the five, he's going to score! Touchdown, Black and Gold! The Mountaineers take the lead with nine minutes left in the game."

Fired up now, the defense stopped every attempt by the Panthers to retake the lead. And on offense, Richardson picked up most of his meager 51 yards running out the clock.

Fans poured out onto the field to congratulate the Black and Gold on winning the first-ever national championship for Appalachian and the first national championship to be won by a North Carolina college football team.

After the game, a reporter asked Coach Moore what his favorite play of the game was, thinking he would say the fumble recovery for a touchdown. He answered with a big smile, "When my quarterback took a knee to end the ball game.

> Jerry: *It was just great. I haven't ever experienced any-thing like it. Everybody was running around hugging everybody and jumping up and down. It was wonderful. One of the things I really enjoyed was D. J. Campbell came down on the field and picked me up off the ground. D. J. was quarterback on my first*

*Photograph by Mark Mitchell/*Watauga Democrat

Jason Hunter scores the winning touchdown against Northern Iowa after picking up the fumble that Marcus Murrell jarred loose from quarterback Eric Sanders.

team back in 1989. Most of those guys have kept in touch and come back every year.

And I'll tell you something else. A lot of the guys that quit after Sparky left have since come back and told me that was the biggest mistake they ever made. There were around 1,000 former Appalachian players at that game, and they all came down to congratulate us on our big win. It was a once-in-a-lifetime deal and we enjoyed every minute of it.

Another thing that most people don't know is all the studying our players did to keep up their classwork. Players were taking exams right up until kickoff of the championship game. The administration and professors were really great. Our academic advisors made sure the players studied and could take their exams. They even delayed the graduation ceremony, and Richie Williams limped across the stage to receive his degree in graphic arts two hours after he was injured in our play-off win over Furman.

He wasn't the only one. Marcus Murrell, a finance and banking major, had two final exams and three presentations during the play-offs. Brandon Turner, an industrial and drafting design major, had a Tuesday morning exam before we left that night for Chattanooga. Corey Lynch, a physics major, had exams during the play-offs. I could go on and on. These kids are not only great football players but are serious students who want to make a difference in life, and we do everything we can to help them do that.

The honors kept flowing in from fans, the media, and even the North Carolina General Assembly. The Mountaineers appeared in both the House and Senate chambers. Several Appalachian players were escorted onto the floor of the chambers. Zach Johnson, who made the team as a walk-on, carried the Division I-AA championship trophy. Walking with him was Brian Stokes who had served as a Marine in Iraq, where he won a Purple Heart.

Coach Jerry Moore gave a stirring speech and reminded the House members that their work in Raleigh could have an impact on people, much like his team's national title victory. He concluded with his favorite quote: "People may not remember who you are or what you say, but they will always remember how you made them feel."

*Photograph by Mark Mitchell/*Watauga Democrat

Richie Williams acknowledges fans during an ESPN interview after his heroic leadership. While playing on a severely injured ankle, he carried the Mountaineers to their first national championship against Northern Iowa.

*Photograph by Marie Freeman/*Watauga Democrat

Coach Moore celebrates Appalachian State's first national championship with his players in 2005.

After all the speeches, the atmosphere grew lighter as some House members recalled their college days. House Speaker Jim Black was a 1958 graduate of Lenoir-Rhyne back when they and Appalachian were fierce rivals. He related how buckets of water were mysteriously dumped on Appalachian State supporters from a dormitory while they toured the campus.

"I want to take this opportunity to apologize; I directed that operation," he said to peals of laughter from the chamber members.

But the most satisfying recognition was the annual awards banquet given for the black-and-gold Mountaineers when they were presented with their highly coveted championship rings. A sold-out crowd of more than 700 witnessed the ring presentation. Coach Moore received his ring last and closed the evening with another motivational speech. He recognized the invaluable role that so many people had in the run to the national title, from his players and assistant coaches to support staff and administration.

There was still one more awards ceremony connected to Appalachian's championship win—Coach of the Year for Division I-AA Region 2. It was the third time Coach Moore had received the award. He had won it back-to-back in 1994 and 1995 when Appalachian was undefeated in Southern Conference play. The American Football Coaches Association named Jerry Moore Coach of the Year and he was also recognized as the winningest coach in Southern Conference history, with 140 victories against only 37 defeats.

Appalachian State University's administration showed its gratitude by extending Moore's contract for three additional years with a hefty salary increase. In announcing the extension, athletic director Charlie Cobb said, "I am proud to tell you that Coach Moore and his entire staff will be back to defend their national championship.

"Coach Moore's leadership," Cobb continued, "has not only taken our football program to heights never reached before, but he has been a terrific ambassador for the athletics department, the university, and the entire High Country community throughout his 17 years in Boone.

> Margaret: *All that recognition was really a wonderful ending for a year that hadn't started out very well. All the turmoil we*

*Photograph by Marie Freeman/*Watauga Democrat

Sharing with fans back in Boone, Coach Moore displays a plaque presented to the Appalachian State Mountaineers by the North Carolina General Assembly. They were congratulated for winning their first national championship and being the only university in North Carolina to win a national football title.

*Photograph by Marie Freeman/*Watauga Democrat

Wayne Norman *(left)* and Brian Stokes both served a combat tour of duty in Iraq as Marines. They walked on after Coach Moore opened the door and invited them to try out.

went through during those dark days after the 2004 season, not knowing if Jerry was going to get fired, seems like a long time ago. But not so long ago that I don't remember how some people acted towards Jerry.

I heard about the awful things that were said about Jerry through friends, who would come up to me at church or downtown shopping and say, "We're thinking of you and support you."

I didn't always feel comfortable when I was out in the community, knowing how some people felt. Our friends and church really supported us and we put it all in God's hands.

BACK-TO-BACK
NATIONAL CHAMPIONS

Jerry: *After our first championship, we knew we had targets on our backs. Everybody would be coming at us with their best shot, starting with an ACC team. N.C. State got our feet back down on the ground. It's the same deal we had in '05. Another tough schedule; there just aren't any easy games. There were several other teams like Wofford, Georgia Southern, and our biggest rival, Furman, that were capable of winning the conference championship. But I was glad to see folks had confidence in us to repeat, like our local sports editor, Steve Behr. He's followed us pretty close for years; maybe he knew something we didn't.*

We wanted the team to enjoy their championship. They worked hard and earned it. I didn't want it to be all work, books, and no fun. We get our players involved in the community as much as we can. They don't always want to go visit the old folks' home, but when we get there they don't have any problem talking to the people. On the way back to campus they always tell me how much they enjoyed it.

We had a kid named Sean Jackson a few years ago that was the smallest player in the Southern Conference. He was listed at 5-6 and 155 pounds. I really don't think he was over 5-4 and

*150 pounds soaking wet. One day I took him down to an elemen-
tary school to talk to the kids. When I saw him with those kids, I
started laughing. He had finally met somebody his own size. He
came in as a partial qualifier because of his low SAT scores. He's
a good example of a kid who worked hard in the classroom and
on the field to become a success. That is what we want for all our
players, to not only be successful on the football field, but a success
in life after football.*

With the team still glowing from their first national championship, Coach Moore and his staff worked hard to bring them back down
to earth. The pursuit for another championship under the new banner of Division I Football Championship Subdivision began with early
morning workouts in March. Cheers and applause from their awards
banquet were still resonating in the players' ears, until the whistle of
the first 6:00 A.M. drills snapped them back to reality.

The expectations of the fans were as high as the blue Appalachian skies. A little taste of success made them hungry for more. There
was no question that Trey Elder would be the Mountaineers' starting
quarterback. After his play-off-winning performance in relief of injured Richie Williams against Furman, everyone had him penciled in
on their program.

The new season with so much hype and promise began badly in
Raleigh. On second down of the Mountaineers' first possession, the
snap sailed over Trey Elder's head and into the end zone where he fell
on it to avert a Wolfpack touchdown. ASU traded touchdowns with
State but went into the half trailing 16-10. Bad field position and N.C.
State's aggressive defense kept the Mountaineers out of their end zone
the second half and turned back the Black and Gold's attempts for an
upset. True freshman Armanti Edwards relieved Elder after the game
was already decided 23-10.

Next up for the Mountaineers was 2004 Division I-AA national champion James Madison. The meeting was billed as the game of
champions and was expected to determine the next champion. An injury to Elder on their first drive brought Armanti Edwards into the
game sooner than Coach Moore had planned. On his first touch of the
ball, Edwards slipped through the Dukes' defense from the seven-yard
line for Appalachian's first score.

*Photograph by Bill Sheffield/*Watauga Democrat

Trey Elder rolls out against N.C. State as the starting quarterback in 2006 after his performances filling in for injured Richie Williams in the 2005 play-off victories against Furman and Northern Iowa.

Elder came back in later, but Edwards saw considerably more action against James Madison than against N.C. State. Kevin Richardson scored two touchdowns while the defense shut down the Dukes' high-powered offense for a 21-10 win against the former champs. The win, however, sparked a controversy over who was going to be the starting quarterback—junior Trey Elder or true freshman Armanti Edwards? Coach Moore hedged when asked by reporters who would be the starter against Mars Hill, a nonconference opponent.

> Jerry: *We knew Trey was going to be our starter, based on his play in the '05 play-off game with Furman that got us to the championship. And he played well in the championship game, no question about that.*
>
> *Armanti was a tall, skinny kid who weighed about 165*

pounds. But he picked up our system well because he ran the same system in high school. It just took him a few weeks in fall practice to learn our terms that were different than he was used to. He had played well in practice and we put him in toward the end of the N.C. State game to get a taste of a big game.

We were going to play him some in the first half against James Madison. When Trey took a hard shot to the head on a roughing call, we had to send him in. He scored the first time he touched the ball. He showed a lot of poise for a freshman and helped us beat a really good team.

After that game, we had a decision to make. We didn't want to get into one of those deals where we shuttled our quarterbacks. We wanted to have a starter. Our decision to go with Armanti had nothing to do with Trey's injury. He just got better with each game.

Mickey Matthews [coach of James Madison] and I are both Texas guys and have been good friends since I was at Texas Tech and he was at West Texas State. We talk at least a couple of times a month. After that game, both our coaching staffs critiqued each other's performance. That was a really neat deal. Those conversations probably helped us to make Armanti our starter based on their defensive coaches' assessment of our offense with him running it.

Armanti Edwards was named the new starter and the Mountaineers crushed nonconference foes Mars Hill 41-0 and Gardner-Webb 41-6 before returning to conference play. The spread offense was clicking on all cylinders with Edwards and Richardson leading the scoring parade. Going into the game against Wofford—another former champion—the Mountaineers were averaging 35 points a game. Armanti had picked up the offense where Richie Williams left off.

The Mountaineers had reeled off five straight wins, four of them blowouts, steamrolling along, scoring an average of 40 points a game. They ran into trouble with Wofford at The Rock, however. Four turnovers and a determined Terriers' defense put the brakes on the Edwards-and-Richardson scoring machine. The Mountaineers scored two early touchdowns in the first quarter and held on to escape with a 14-7 win.

Coach Moore told reporters in his postgame news conference, "You're not going to go out there and thump everybody every time. I'm going to tell you, Wofford is a solid football team. Their defense is disciplined and they don't like to give up big plays. We made a lot of mistakes on offense. We have to correct those kinds of things. We were really lucky to win one turning it over four times."

The turnover bug followed Appalachian to Statesboro. The Mountaineers once again had to overcome multiple turnovers that allowed Georgia Southern two touchdowns. Appalachian came from behind to tie the game and send it into overtime. It took two overtimes for the Mountaineers to finally wrestle the game away from the Eagles 27-20.

After the second consecutive game in which the Mountaineers lost four turnovers, Coach Moore was more than a little concerned. "We're not going to run up a flag over it," Moore said to postgame reporters. "You bet we're concerned. You don't turn your head on it. You've got to address the issue and get it corrected. It could have very easily cost us a ball game Saturday."

Quarterback Amanti Edwards was more blunt in his assessment of the offensive turnovers. "If it hadn't been for our defense, we would have lost the last two games," Edwards told reporters after the game.

Appalachian still had their old rival Furman to deal with after two games in which the offense struggled before finally taking home wins. The Paladins came to The Rock ranked No. 6 with plans to knock off No. 1 Appalachian State. It began like so many games in the past, a defensive struggle with neither side giving up much ground.

With the score tied 7-7, Furman was threatening to score with time running out before the half. The Paladins attempted a go-ahead field goal. All-American Corey Lynch blocked the kick, recovered it, and ran it back 79 yards for a touchdown. The play ended the half with Appalachian leading 14-7 and the momentum swung to the Mountaineers in the second half. The offense and defense found their rhythm again and shut Furman out while lighting up the scoreboard for a 40-7 thrashing of the Purple Paladins.

"You never dream that a Furman-Appalachian game would be decided by that margin," Coach Moore said. "I was proud of the way we played. We got behind 7-0 and we talked about doing things yourself because nobody was going to help you."

The Mountaineers' championship express was back on track. They clinched a second consecutive Southern Conference Championship when they crushed Western Carolina 31-10. Appalachian's 10-1 record meant they would defend their championship title at home at The Rock.

For the play-off games at home that would return them to Chattanooga, Appalachian resumed the bulldozing attack they used to destroy opponents before the Wofford game. The Mountaineers' scoring machine and stingy defense swept the play-offs as they crushed Coastal Carolina 45-28, Montana State 38-17, and Youngstown State 49-24 in successive weeks on their way to meet the University of Massachusetts to defend their title.

2006 National Championship—University of Massachusetts

"One Moore Time," announced the *Watauga Democrat*'s bold special edition headline. The UMass Minutemen led the nation in rush defense, limiting opponents to 101 yards a game. Kevin Richardson didn't get the message. He gained 179 of the 285 rushing yards that shredded UMass' vaunted defense. The Minutemen's strategy backfired. Their plan was to use their bruising running back Steve Baylark to soften up Appalachian's defense and then go in for the kill in the fourth quarter against the tired Mountaineers. It was the Appalachian offense that wore down the Minutemen's defense.

Clinging to a 21-17 lead late in the fourth quarter, Appalachian drove 80 yards in 14 plays, running the clock down to only 1:51 when Richardson crossed the goal line for his fourth touchdown of the night. Most of the crowd of 22,808, who were dressed in black and gold, roared their approval. Richardson's efforts set a new single-season rushing record at 1,676 yards, including 30 touchdowns. That drive closed the door on UMass, 28-17.

The Minutemen's quarterback Liam Coen didn't give up. He tried to move downfield with long passes for a quick score. Corey Lynch got in front of the UMass receiver for career No. 18 interception to end the game. It was Lynch's second major defensive play of the game. Earlier he chased down Brad Listorti, who thought he was headed for his second touchdown. Lynch's effort held Listorti to a 40-yard gain

*Photograph by Marie Freeman/*Watauga Democrat

Kevin Richardson sprints for one of his four touchdowns against University of Massachusetts in the Mountaineers' second straight championship victory, 28-17.

*Photograph by Marie Freeman/*Watauga Democrat

Team-leading pass defender Corey Lynch breaks up a pass against University of Massachusetts in the Mountaineers' 2006 championship victory. (Note a heavily padded brace is protecting Corey's broken right elbow.)

instead of a touchdown and forced the Minutemen to settle for a field goal that preserved Appalachian's 21-17 lead.

After the game Coach Moore praised his star safety. "When I think about Corey, I think about the courage he's got. He's got one screw in his arm that's about the size of a pencil and is two inches long and a metal plate with six other screws. Yet he was already talking about playing in the first round of the play-offs when he got out of the hospital."

Lynch had broken his arm six weeks earlier in the Citadel game and only missed two games of the season. The team physician released the defensive standout for the second-round game against Montana State.

The final whistle sent thousands of black-and-gold-clad fans onto the field as they celebrated with their team who had just won back-to-back national championships. The temperature was near freezing by the end of the game. Neither the victorious Appalachian Mountaineers nor their delirious fans, who danced around on the field, hugging and backslapping everyone in sight, seemed to notice.

The victory over Massachusetts set a school record of 14 straight wins after a loss to N.C. State in their opener. Appalachian dominated the Southern Conference with a high-octane offense that averaged 35 points a game, while a stingy defense only gave up 14 points. Appalachian's powerhouse finished the season with the second-longest home winning streak in the country at 27 games, behind the University of Southern California.

This achievement was accomplished after the tumultuous months between the winter of 2004 and the summer of 2005, when Coach Jerry Moore steadied an athletic department that was in trouble and disarray. He was dedicated to the Appalachian athletic program and made the transition to a new chancellor and athletic director a smooth-working operation. At the same time, he laid the foundation for his team's future success.

Jerry: UMass was a great win for us, no doubt about it. We had worked all season with that big target on our backs and everyone wanting to know if we could win back-to-back championships. I tried to be positive about it but didn't dwell on it with our players. I know it was always in the backs of the players' and coaches' minds; we just didn't talk about it until the time came. After we beat Youngstown State, we concentrated our full attention on UMass and winning our second championship.

Our fans were great; they have really supported us. Every time I went downtown someone wanted to know if we were going to three-peat. The championships have really revitalized Boone and Appalachian State. It's just been great to see how everyone got caught up in it. People in other states know who we are, and it has helped our recruiting. We had some big holes to fill on our line the next year. We had to keep bringing in new players that could contribute right away. We signed some good players that helped us tremendously in the 2007 season.

MOUNTAINEERS BRING DOWN
THE BIG HOUSE

Jerry: *When Charlie* [Cobb] *came down to my office to tell me of the possibility of playing Michigan, I jumped at it. He came back several times after that to make sure I really wanted to play a Big 10 powerhouse like Michigan. I told him absolutely, with no hesitation. It would be a great experience for our team and give our program a lot of good exposure. After we looked at the tapes that summer before spring ball, I told the other coaches that I believed we could play with those guys.*

One day, getting dressed out for spring practice, our quarterback, Armanti Edwards, came up to me and asked if we were really going to play Michigan. I told him not to worry; they put their pants on one leg at a time just like he did. He looked at me, and said, "But Coach, they wear 48 longs!"

We all laughed, but I was serious. I felt like we had the talent to stay in the game with them. The team proved on the field what I felt all along, with one of the biggest upsets in football history. After that game and all the notoriety, we had a target on our backs so big you could see it a mile away. Everybody was gunning for us.

Margaret: *When Jerry came home that day last spring and said, "Margaret, how would you like to go to the Big House?" I answered, "Sure, that would be great. Are you talking about the White House in Washington, D.C.?"*

He said, "No, I'm talking about the University of Michigan. That's what they call their stadium. It holds 109,000 people and we are going to play them there our first game."

He was so excited about playing a really great team in front of that many people, I couldn't believe it. He said they would be a top-ranked team and they packed that big stadium every home game. Who would have thought we would beat them in their own stadium? It was really an emotional game. My hands were shaking so bad I couldn't hold my binoculars still on that last play when Corey blocked their field-goal try.

It was such a big upset with all the national coverage. I really felt sorry for Coach Lloyd Carr's wife after the game. I understood how she must have felt. Just knowing what was going on here in Boone, I can only imagine what was going on up there. We knocked them completely out of the national ratings; that must have been tough to take. I sat down and wrote her a letter as soon as we got home.

With two straight national championships under Appalachian's belt and 13 starters—10 of them seniors—returning for the 2007 season, Boone was all abuzz with excitement. Walking in downtown Boone on King Street, black-and-gold Appalachian T-shirts and bumper stickers were everywhere. Coach Moore said a man came up to him and held up two tickets to the Michigan game.

Jerry: *I'd like to have a nickel for every time I heard the term "three-peat" before the season even started. Everybody was asking if were going to three-peat when I went anywhere. Just walking around town or at the grocery store, no matter where I went, everybody asked.*

When asked if he minded all the talk about a three-peat, Coach Moore said, "Shoot no, everybody was just excited to get the season started, and so were we. A lot of people talked about the national attention that winning the championships brought to our school. That's a neat thing to experience here in Boone. People really wanted to identify with our team.

Moore's program had been good for a long time; 17 of his 18 teams had winning records. The previous two years, the Mountaineers blossomed into back-to-back national champions. In spite of what some of his detractors said back in 2004, Jerry Moore's coaching had only gotten better. The loyal coaching staff had been around an average of nine years, except for defensive coordinator John Wiley, who came up with Moore from Texas in 1989.

This was a new season, however, with three of their four down linemen graduated off the two-championship defense. Returning were record-setting and All-Conference quarterback Armanti Edwards along with All-Conference and ASU record-breaking Kevin Richardson at tailback. Seven starters on offense and six on defense would return.

Moore and his staff were challenged to fill in the holes. As usual, Moore had a stable of talented freshmen and sophomores waiting for their chance to make the starting team. Their goal was the same as the veterans: return to Chattanooga for an unprecedented third national championship.

Senior All-Conference center Scott Suttle said it best: "It's an even bigger bull's-eye on us this year, but I think we're expecting even more of ourselves."

When September 1 rolled around, it was time to put away all the talk of the last two championships. The Mountaineers were going to the Big House. The University of Michigan's gargantuan stadium was the largest football stadium in the country, and it was sold out every home game to watch the winningest program in college football.

Jerry: *Yeah, they were big and fast and have probably the longest winning tradition in college football. But we have a winning tradition, too, and we prepare the same way we do every week and every year for each team we play. We usually keep the team together the night before a game and watch an inspirational movie. We planned to watch the* Miracle on Ice *movie about the American Olympic hockey team that beat the Russians that we watched before playing Northern Iowa and UMass for the championships.*

We had our projectionist rig it up so the beginning of the Miracle movie would start first. You could hear the guys, especially the seniors groan a little. Then the movie Invincible came on. They cheered. It's a true story about thirty-year-old Vince Papale who was down on his luck as a part-time teacher and part-time bartender who made it as a walk-on for the Philadelphia Eagles. What are the odds of that happening in the NFL? But we have a history of successful walk-ons. There were four starters and All-Conference players that played for us as walk-ons. They could really identify with the movie and really enjoyed it.

Inspirational movies and speakers are just some of the ways we try to help our players get their feet on the ground and mentor them. Another thing the players have done under the leadership of Nic Cardwell, Corey Lynch, and Billy Riddle, before he left on a mission trip to Africa, was to form a weekly Bible study. We don't preach at the guys or anything like that, but we are here as role models for these young men.

We form a voluntary prayer circle holding hands before each game. We are trying to help build successful student athletes and young men of character so when they get out in the world they will be prepared for whatever comes up. I can't say that we have ever had divine intervention in any of our games, as some newspapers have, but it sure doesn't hurt to try.

Michigan had never played a lower Division I FCS team before, but Coach Lloyd Carr didn't see any risk in playing Appalachian. The Wolverines had won 11 consecutive games the previous season and were picked fifth in the preseason poll.

"We had the benefit of watching all of Appalachian's games from last fall," Michigan Coach Carr said. "We knew their strengths from the standpoint of their speed and integrating a great athlete at quarterback who was a threat and who touches the ball on every play."

More than 20,000 black-and-gold-clad fans poured into the Big House for the long-awaited start of the assault on a third championship. The players looked like ants running around the field to the visitors in the upper sections, but the fans were proud to be there to make some noise for the Mountaineers.

> Jerry: *I got chills coming out of the tunnel and trotting onto the field in front of all those people and hearing our fans cheering for us. I've never seen anything like it; it was awesome. That was an experience I will remember the rest of my life. And for some of our freshmen, who were playing high-school ball this time last year, it was beyond anything they could have ever imagined.*

> Margaret: *We were pretty far up and had to use binoculars to see the guys. But they didn't look excited at all. They were so calm as they went through their warmup drills. I think Jerry was more nervous than they were. I wasn't nervous until the Michigan team came out. They were huge and they just kept coming out of that tunnel. Then I got nervous.*

Michigan scored on their opening drive, but the Mountaineers weren't intimidated. Appalachian came right back on its first possession and showcased its speed as Dexter Jackson gathered in a short pass over the middle and turned it into a 68-yard touchdown. The Wolverines held Appalachian in check the rest of the first quarter. But the Mountaineers went on a three-touchdown rampage in the second quarter and shut Michigan out until the last 16 seconds before the half when the Wolverines managed a field goal to make it 28-17.

The reality of the speed and skills of Appalachian began to sink in to a stunned Michigan team as they headed to the dressing room. While the score was still 28-14, a Michigan security guard on the sidelines turned to Randy Jackson, WKBC sideline reporter and the father of ASU play-by-play announcer David Jackson, and asked, "Didn't your guys get the memo? You're not supposed to win."

The second half saw Michigan make a big comeback against the tiring Mountaineers who only used 35 players the entire game. Julian Rauch's field goal kept the Mountaineers in the lead until late in the fourth quarter. A pair of Michigan touchdowns nudged the Wolverines into the lead, 32-31, after the Mountaineer defense denied both of Michigan's two-point conversion attempts.

The Mountaineer offense stepped it up a notch. They fought their

Photograph courtesy of Watauga Democrat

Armanti Edwards followed Dexter Jackson's shocking 68-yard touchdown catch-and-run play with a scoring dive over Michigan's offensive line. Edwards' score triggered a three touchdown barrage by the Mountaineers that had Michigan reeling at halftime.

Photograph courtesy of Watauga Democrat

Julian Rauch calmly kicked one of the most important field goals of his career to defeat Michigan 34-32. Corey Lynch preserved the stunning upset by blocking Michigan's field-goal attempt with only five seconds remaining in the game.

way down to a first and goal on the Michigan five-yard line with 30 seconds left and no timeouts. Coach Moore decided to go for the field goal rather than risk a turnover or run out of time. Rauch's 24-yard kick split the uprights for a 34-32 lead.

In their hurry-up 30-second drill after the kickoff, Michigan's Heisman candidate, Chad Henne, completed a 46-yard pass to the Mountaineers' 20-yard line. With only six seconds showing on the clock the Wolverines lined up for a field-goal attempt. It was a 37-yard attempt, well within their kicker's range.

All-American safety Corey Lynch lined up wide outside the left side of the Michigan line. On the snap of the ball, Lynch streaked in untouched and blocked the kick with his chest. The ball took an Appalachian bounce and Lynch quickly scooped the ball up in stride and headed for Michigan's goal line. Fatigue and leg cramps slowed the league-leading kick blocker down and he was shoved out of bounds on the five-yard line as time expired.

"It sounded like a volcano erupting on our sideline when Corey blocked that kick and picked it up to try and score," Moore said. Then pandemonium broke out from the 20,000-plus Appalachian fans who poured down from the stadium onto the playing field as nearly 90,000 Michigan fans stood in shocked silence. There was jubilation all over the field as reporters swarmed around the Mountaineers.

"I really wanted to score at the Big House," said the game's hero, Corey Lynch. He joked about the late-game heroics and said, "That's our plan every game to keep App State fans interested." They had managed to do that almost every week the previous two seasons. Later, when asked if he thought that the win over No. 5–ranked Michigan should get the Mountaineers ranked in the Division I FBS polls, Lynch said, "I think we just proved it today." Lynch was proven correct as the FBS voted to change their rules to include FCS teams in their rankings two days after the big upset. The rule became known as the "Appalachian State Rule." And the Mountaineers enjoyed a brief FCS ranking in the top 25.

The monster win brought a media blitz to Boone like none other. Immediately after the game, celebrating students stormed Kidd Brewer Stadium, took down a goalpost, and paraded it around campus. When the bus arrived from the Tri-Cities airport, a crowd of 10,000 students and fans, still celebrating, were gathered at Kidd Brewer Stadium to greet their giant slayers.

The High Country's *Watauga Democrat* ran a special edition—"The Anatomy of an Upset"—loaded with photos of the game and celebrating students carrying a goalpost down the street on campus. The *Winston-Salem Journal's* "Mountaineers Win One for the Ages" ran atop Sunday's sports page. The greatest national recognition of the Mountaineers' feat was the *Sports Illustrated* story and cover photo of Dexter Jackson streaking for a touchdown with the title "Alltime Upset: Appalachian State Stuns No. 5 Michigan."

Issues of the magazine flew off the shelves everywhere in the High Country and the rest of western North Carolina. Local fans were forced to call relatives in other states to get copies of the upset of all time. Coach Moore was said to have a big stack of *Sports Illustrated* magazines on his desk to sign for proud fans. His secretary, Denise, indicated it would probably be Christmas break before he could get them all signed.

Jerry: *I was really proud of the way our team played. They really played well. Sometimes playing well isn't enough, but our guys really laid it out there on the field. I was especially proud of our defense, going with three new starters. But I told them in the locker room right after the game to enjoy this, but not to forget we had a game next week against Lenoir-Rhyne. Our situations were reversed. Lenoir-Rhyne was just coming up from Division II and had nothing to lose. And you know sometimes big underdogs do win. We knocked Michigan out of the top 25, but they came back. They are a really good football team.*

We couldn't afford to let our guard down and take Lenoir-Rhyne too lightly. We had a tough conference schedule with all but one or two teams really equal. We couldn't afford a loss if we wanted to win the conference championship for a third straight season. That's what we work so hard for every practice and the last two years; it's really paid off.

The euphoria lasted for weeks, at least in the minds of the black-and-gold fans. Home-game attendance soared to over 28,000 for the

Lenoir-Rhyne game that was a mismatch. Trey Elder, who started for Armanti Edwards who was resting a sprained shoulder, threw four touchdown passes. The Mountaineers never missed a beat, scoring on their first six possessions and rolling to a 48-7 win.

> Jerry: *I was pleased with the way our players responded after the unprecedented media attention. Our guys handled it great. We were glad to be playing at home after traveling up to Michigan. We were really beaten up. Armanti had a shoulder bruise and we rested him for several weeks until conference play started, because we had complete faith in Trey.*
>
> *The greatest thing about playing at home is our fans. The crowds were awesome. I've been in a lot of big stadiums and around some unbelievable crowds, but cramming over 28,000 fans into a 16,500-seat stadium just shows how much respect our people have for our school and football program.*

The Mountaineers extended their home winning streak to 29 after finishing off determined Northern Arizona 34-21. That ended nonconference play. "This is where it starts," Moore said in a pregame press conference. "Thank goodness it's here, that's what we've been looking forward to. We've had some pretty neat distractions and we're not used to all that stuff. It starts counting this week, though.

"We had a close game with Wofford last year and don't expect anything less this year. Mike Ayers is a good friend of mine and he has a really good program down there. His teams are always disciplined and play hard."

Facing Wofford, one of the consistently competitive members of the Southern Conference, would be a big test for the No. 1–ranked Mountaineers. ASU went down to Spartanburg, South Carolina, and met an inspired Terrier team that had lost its opening game to N.C. State. Wofford's option running attack chewed up 431 yards of Mountaineer real estate and forced three turnovers. When the clock ran out, the Terriers had hung a 42-31 defeat on the Mountaineers, which snapped its FCS-leading 17-game winning streak.

Following Wofford with Elon was no break for the Mountaineers. The young Phoenix team had joined the Southern Conference only in 2003 but had made its presence felt every year. Freshman quarterback

Scott Riddle filled the air with passes at the rate of 343 yards a game.

It was a completely different situation than Wofford with their grinding ground game. The game was a shootout for the first half. Mountaineer special teams broke down and allowed a kickoff return of 83 yards to set up a score. A 100-yard kickoff return for a touchdown kept the Phoenix in the game.

Appalachian's defense stiffened and the offense found its rhythm, which helped the Mountaineers pull ahead by scoring five touchdowns in six possessions for a 49-32 win. Trey Elder once again started in place of Armanti Edwards, who aggravated his shoulder in the loss to Wofford. Elder led a 526-yard assault against Elon, including three scoring runs of his own.

An easy 45-7 homecoming win over Gardner-Webb and an open date the following week was a welcomed relief for the banged-up Mountaineers.

*Photograph by Mark Mitchell/*Watauga Democrat

Devon Moore, Kevin Richardson's heir apparent, breaks into the clear to help the Mountaineers in a vital 49-32 victory over Elon to stay in play-off contention.

Jerry: *The open date came at a good time for us. Sometimes you hate to break the rhythm and momentum and all that stuff, but we needed an open date for a lot of reasons. We had a bunch of injuries in the weeks after the Michigan game. And we needed it to put more distance between the distractions from the Michigan win and all the media attention. We had a lot of work to do to get ready for the rest of the conference schedule. We needed it about as much mentally as we did physically.*

Rested and raring to go again, the Mountaineers hosted another tough Southern Conference opponent in Georgia Southern at The Rock. High-scoring games had become routine in the conference that year. Most of the top-tier teams had averaged 35 or 40 points a game, and this contest was no exception. Thirty-five total points were scored in the first quarter, but Appalachian's offense was stymied until late in the fourth quarter. The Mountaineers scored back-to-back touchdowns to close the gap to 38-35 with 1:10 left in the game.

Appalachian stopped the Bulldogs and forced a punt. Dexter Jackson returned the kick 45 yards to the Bulldogs' 20-yard line, but a penalty brought the ball back to the ASU 36-yard line. The Mountaineers had no timeouts. When they got near field-goal range again, an illegal chop block penalty moved them out of field-goal range. Appalachian's drive stalled as time ran out. It was a loss the Mountaineers couldn't afford if they wanted in the play-offs. The loss also broke the Mountaineers' 30 game-winning streak. Appalachian had not lost at The Rock since Maine squeaked by 14-13 in the first round of 2002 play-offs.

Jerry: *When Dexter Jackson took that punt back inside their 20-yard line, I wasn't even thinking field goal. I thought we would score and win the game. Then I saw that flag lying there. It was a tough deal. I watched replays, but there wasn't a conclusive view of the illegal block. That was a tough one to lose. That gave us two conference loses and hurt our chances of getting into the play-offs. I didn't know what to say to the team in the locker room. The coach is supposed to say something uplifting like a Zig Zigler, but I was just as hurt as they were. It was really hard.*

With archrival Furman coming up, the Mountaineers had to put the Georgia Southern loss behind them in a hurry. The conference was so balanced that seven teams were still in the running for at least a share of a Southern Conference Championship with four weeks remaining in the regular season.

> Jerry: *We went into the Furman game with a skeleton crew. The offensive line was especially hard hit with two day-by-day probable returns and two that were definitely out. The defense had some dings, too. It was a bad situation for our defense that had allowed 37 points in three conference games. The game pitted the two national touchdown leaders at tailback. I think Richardson had 58 scores, one more than Felton.*
>
> *The game lived up to its billing and our history of close, hard-fought games. Corey Lynch, like he had so many times in his career, saved the game for us and kept us in the hunt.*

Statistically the winner of the Furman game would stay in the championship race for one more week. Both teams with 1-2 conference records needed a win.

The Mountaineers came out strong early and rolled up a 24-7 lead at halftime. The Black and Gold had to hang on the second half to preserve its lead. The Paladins were driving for what could have tied the score with 1:11 left in the game. Quarterback Renaldo Gray worked his team down within the 30-yard line in Mountaineer territory. With the final seconds ticking off the clock, Gray spotted his receiver Patrick Sprague in Appalachian's end zone and lofted a pass for the fade route in the corner. The game lived up to the Appalachian versus Furman reputation of nerve-racking, last-second endings. Always reliable Corey Lynch leaped in front of the receiver like he had done so many times before. His interception ended the game, preserving the Mountaineer's 34-27 win.

"We had been losing the first quarter," Armanti Edwards said after the game. "We wanted to come out and take it down the field and score; we didn't want to play catch up against a good team like Furman."

> Jerry: *After the Furman win, that Citadel game was critical for us. Armanti was awesome; he ran for almost 300 yards and passed for two touchdowns. That left four teams tied for first*

*Photograph by Mark Mitchell/*Watauga Democrat

Armanti Edwards pulls away from The Citadel defense in the Mountaineers' 45-24 victory, which started Edwards on his way to a team rushing record of 1,727 yards.

place after that game. We were in the hunt and felt good about our chances with Western Carolina and Chattanooga left on our schedule.

Appalachian's new offensive attitude, about coming out fast at the opening gun, paid huge dividends against The Citadel. Quarterback Armanti Edwards led the way as the Mountaineers amassed 580 total yards. Edwards' swift feet carried him for a team record 291 of those rushing yards and he passed for another 148 yards.

"There was a lot open, especially when we ran the speed option," Armanti said to postgame reporters. "They blitzed a lot but keyed on defending the pitch instead of me. I knew if we could get it to the secondary, we could break it all the way."

In the first quarter, Edwards broke for an untouched 80-yard touchdown run to blow the game open early. The Citadel played without injured star quarterback Duran Lawson and couldn't keep up with the fleet Mountaineer offense. Appalachian State cruised to a 45-24 win.

After the game a jubilant Mountaineer team whooped it up when they learned that Elon and Wofford both had lost, creating a four-way tie for first place among Elon, Wofford, Georgia Southern, and Appalachian State. Everyone had at least two losses. The Mountaineers had the advantage of playing their last two games at home against the two weakest teams in the conference.

The Mountaineers held a lopsided lead in the 72-year-old traditional battle for the Old Mountain Jug. Appalachian had held the Jug for 16 of the 18 years Jerry Moore had coached at The Rock. In 2004, the Western Carolina Catamounts wrestled the jug away from the Mountaineers in a game that brought a lot of criticism down on Moore and his staff. As a result, he installed the new offense that had been so successful. Averaging 35 points a game with the new formation, ASU caught the eye of several other teams in the conference that later adopted a variation of Moore's new system.

> Jerry: *No matter how many times we have beaten Western Carolina, I told our players they couldn't overlook anyone, especially with so much at stake. I reminded them of the 1994 game when we played VMI at home and lost to a 0-10 team. It knocked us out of the play-offs. The Western game was the same situation; we had to beat them to stay in the race, to at least tie for the championship, and hopefully win home-field advantage.*

So much for all the worry about Western Carolina upsetting the Mountaineers. Appalachian came out smoking and scored on its first eight possessions. In doing so, the Mountaineers set a modern-day school record in the 79-35 romp. The defense created five turnovers giving the ball back to Armanti and company. Kevin Richardson raced for a career high 215 yards and added two scores to his league-leading 60 touchdowns. Corey Lynch delivered the final blow with career interception number 21, which he returned for a 65-yard touchdown.

> Jerry: *I told Kent* [Briggs, Western Carolina's coach] *after the game that I didn't like to score a bunch of points like that. We got some interceptions and fumble recoveries that went for touchdowns and it just got out of hand.*
>
> *We had several of our defensive backup guys hurt and had*

to leave the starters in the whole game. We weren't trying to run up the score. To be honest, we didn't want to celebrate too soon at the half because Western came back against Wofford and scored 41 points in the second half. They didn't win, but that was a lot of points against a really good Wofford team.

We scored a lot of points, but our defense gave up 31 points and that continued to concern us. Not many teams in the league were playing good defense and everybody was scoring a lot of points. Our young defensive players were getting better with each game, but that's something you can't rush. We just had to keep working hard, trying to get better.

THREE-PEAT—
MOORE MOUNTAIN MAGIC

Jerry: *We had our work cut out for us against James Madi-son. Mickey Matthews [the James Madison coach] and I talked at the end of the season last year and hoped we wouldn't have to play each other in the play-offs, but maybe in the championship game. That would have been great. But when the pairings came out, there we were, matched against them in the first round.*

Mickey and I are good friends and go back a long way to when we were both coaching in Texas. He has a great program at James Madison and is always a tough opponent. They came down here last year and played us a real good game. We were fortunate to come away with a win. I'm sure they haven't forgotten that loss and will be looking for some payback.

First-round play-off at The Rock—James Madison

The season was over and the Mountaineers had won their third straight conference championship! James Madison, Appalachian's first play-off opponent, came to The Rock with a little revenge in mind for the 21-10 loss handed them the previous regular season.

The Dukes came to Boone with a 28-point scoring average and

a defense that held opponents to only 212 yards a game. The play-off prognosticators played up the high-flying Mountaineer offense averaging 43 points a game against the rock-solid defense of the Dukes.

The results on the field played out quite differently. James Madison's offense pushed the Mountaineers all over the field and chewed up huge chunks of clock doing it. The Dukes scored first with less than two minutes left in first period and added another score in the second quarter on relentless drives that the Mountaineers couldn't stop.

James Madison shut out the Mountaineers until Edwards broke the ice with one of his patented fake handoffs, then turned it up the middle for a four-yard score. Richardson bulled his way into the end zone to cap the second scoring drive that resulted from a James Madison turnover.

The 14-13 halftime score was much closer than the game statistics showed. "We were really upset at the halftime," James Madison coach Mickey Matthews said. "We thought we fairly well dominated the first half. It was a 13-point swing when they caused our tight end to fumble."

The domination continued in the second half as the Dukes used up a lot of clock and converted third and fourth downs too often for Coach Moore's liking. The two teams swapped scores in the third quarter, but both missed their extra-point tries. Blame it on the 28-degree temperature or aggressive defense—either way, it was unusual to see so many point-after attempts fail.

The crowd of 14,040, dressed mostly in black and gold, were on their feet throughout the game. It was crunch time for the Mountaineers, with hope fading and the Dukes leading 27-19 midway through the fourth quarter. Armanti Edwards drove the offense into field-goal range before stalling. Julian Rauch atoned for his missed extra point in the third quarter by making the 45-yard field goal, drawing the Mountaineers closer at 27-22 with 4:51 remaining.

Appalachian needed another touchdown, but the Mountaineers weren't optimistic about getting the ball back after the Dukes used up nine minutes on their last scoring drive. The Mountaineers' special team swarmed downfield and stopped the Dukes' return man on their 22-yard line with less than four minutes left. All James Madison had to do now was grind out enough first downs to run the clock out.

"We had handled the Mountaineer defensive line all afternoon,"

Coach Matthews said. "I was confident we could control the ball and that we were in control of our play-off destiny."

What happened next baffled every Monday-morning quarterback from the High Country of North Carolina to James Madison's hometown of Harrisburg in Virginia's beautiful Shenandoah Valley. Why did Coach Matthews risk giving the Mountaineers a chance to score the winning touchdown? That question will haunt Coach Matthews the rest of his life.

Following the kickoff after Rauch's field goal, the Dukes' drive stalled on the 31-yard line. It was third and one for a first down. All 14,040 fans were on their feet cheering their teams on. It was a make-or-break play for both teams.

When the teams lined up, Appalachian was showing an eight-man front to stop James Madison's vaunted running attack that had dominated them most of the game. As soon as the ball was snapped, Corey Lynch came screaming in on a safety blitz. Lynch met tailback Jamal Sullivan in the hole with a bone-jarring tackle for a one-yard loss. It was fourth and two.

Without taking a timeout or any hesitation, James Madison lined up in the I-formation. Quarterback Rodney Landers, the Dukes' most prolific ground gainer with 124 yards, lined up under center. Landers called a quick count and tried to sneak it past the first-down marker, but 285-pound defensive lineman Anthony Williams stood Landers up and buried him for no gain. The defense had done its job and the Mountaineers had the ball in easy scoring range. It had to be a touchdown to overcome James Madison's five-point lead.

Appalachian managed only six yards on three tries at the Dukes' line. With the ball resting on the 25-yard line, they had to go for it on fourth down. Armanti Edwards rolled to his left with several Dukes in pursuit. As he was about to be caught, he flicked a pass to Devon Moore who had worked free on the five-yard line. First down, Appalachian!

The Mountaineers faked a screen pass and Edwards tucked the ball under his arm and scampered into the end zone for the score. Rauch, who was having a bad night, missed the extra point, and Appalachian clung to a slim 28-27 lead. Game over? Not quite. James Madison still had almost two minutes to ruin the Mountaineers' dream of a third championship game.

The Dukes moved downfield after the kickoff with a 39-yard pass completion. Three running plays advanced them down to the Mountaineers' nine-yard line. The Mountaineers' tough defense of only a few moments ago was badly beaten and James Madison was only a chip shot away from a 30-28 victory.

In an effort to get their field-goal kicker a better angle, the Dukes sent Jamal Sullivan, who had gained 67 yards on the day, on a sweep towards the center of the field. The first-down stopper on the previous series, Corey Lynch, came up from his safety position and teamed up with Jacque Roman to put a brutal hit on Sullivan. While Lynch and Roman had the ball carrier stopped, Roman punched the ball out. It bounded into open field towards the Appalachian sideline, where the bench was screaming and pointing at the loose ball for a Mountaineer to recover. Pierre Banks raced two James Madison players for the ball and it took a reverse bounce right into his hands.

Pandemonium broke out all over the field and the Mountaineers were flagged for excessive celebration. When order was restored, Edwards took a knee to end the game and the celebration started all over again.

> Jerry: *If Madison had made that first down after our field goal, the ball game would have been over. They had been eating up the clock with long drives all day. It was a gutsy call. I won't try to second guess Mickey on that one. With the success his team had running the ball, I might have made the same call. We had to go for it on fourth down ourselves just four plays later. We were as confident that our offense could make it as Mickey was about his offense. We made it and went on to score the winning touchdown. They didn't make it and lost the game. That's what makes this game so great.*

James Madison devoured 40:20 of the game clock while penetrating Appalachian's defense for 312 yards rushing. Their powerful offense converted 11 of 19 third downs and four of five fourth downs. The one they missed cost them the game. The Mountaineers won the two most important statistics of the game: fumbles recovered and the final score, 28-27.

"I'm really glad it's not a statistical game," Moore said at the postgame news conference, "but a game that you end up with what's on the scoreboard. I hurt for Mickey—I hurt for his team—because we are very close and talk a couple times a month all year long."

Stunned James Madison fans filed slowly and silently out of the stands. Meanwhile Coach Mickey Matthews fielded questions about the two decisions he made in the closing minutes that cost James Madison the game.

"I didn't want to punt because there was enough time for them to score. I knew that there was always the chance we wouldn't make it and give them the ball on our 32-yard line. We had been running at will against them all day. I honestly didn't think they could stop us. We had made four previous fourth-down conversions." Coach Matthews shook his head. "You have to give Appalachian credit; they stopped us when it counted.

"I take full responsibility for the loss. I should never have put Jamal Sullivan in that position. He's a redshirt freshman. With 22 seconds left, I should have known better. I knew they would be grabbing for the ball. It wasn't the kid's fault. It was the coach's mistake. I should have gone ahead and kicked the field goal instead of trying to get the ball closer to the middle of the field. I know better. That's as hard as we've played, and as much as we dominated them, not to have won is disheartening."

At the postgame news conference with Coach Moore, Corey Lynch talked about the game-ending fumble. "I was in on the hit on Sullivan and didn't see the fumble," he said. "I sat up and heard all the yelling and everybody jumping up and down after the recovery. I sat there a minute still mad that we blew a coverage and let them beat us for a 39-yard gain to get down inside our red zone. I take it to heart when I mess things up, especially if I let my teammates down. It was kind of like we got a little help from a higher power to overcome James Madison's offense. God was on the mountain today."

Quarterback Armanti Edwards put it more simply: "It was by the grace of God that we got that fumble, that's all I could think of was the man upstairs."

Coach Moore concluded, "Some people may call it a miracle or luck, but I call it not ever giving up. Our defense was pushed around most of the game. But they hung in there after we were down five points and James Madison had the ball with less than five minutes to play. They held the offense that ran for over 300 yards to no gain on two straight running plays to give the ball back to the offense to win the game. Then they forced a big fumble to protect that 28-27 victory. When I saw Pierre Banks fall on that loose ball, I looked up at the sky, that's the first thing I did. That was awesome."

It wasn't hard to see the influence of Jerry Moore's faith and leadership on his team. Nearly half the team had attended a weekly Bible study on their own initiative for the last three years. Three time All-American safety Corey Lynch, reserve safety Billy Riddle, and tight end Nic Cardwell had been instrumental in nurturing the team's spiritual life. Riddle gave up his senior season to go on a Christian mission to Africa.

> Jerry: *James Madison was one of the toughest games we played all year. Was it a miracle? I don't know, but to win a game like that showed the character of our team. Walking off the field after that game, I couldn't help but think of the grit our guys had. They never gave up and kept chipping away at a really good team to earn the right to play again the next week.*

Quarterfinal—Eastern Washington at The Rock

> Jerry: *When you get to this level they're all good, or they wouldn't be here. When I studied different offenses looking for ideas a few years ago, I checked out Eastern Washington's West Coast–style offense. They didn't do very well last year, but turned it around this year. That big sophomore quarterback makes them go. He was offensive player of the year in their league. He's kinda like a big Armanti.*
>
> *Their offense was more productive this year. They beat Mc-Neese State 44-15. McNeese was unbeaten and the No. 2 seed. You bet they were a terrific football team. They ran neck and neck with us on total offense, but they threw more than we did. Elon was the only team that we had played that passed as much as Eastern did.*
>
> *But our pass defense was really good, and Corey Lynch just had an outstanding game. Our defensive line did a great job containing their running attack. Our offense did some really good*

things, too. They made some plays when we needed them. But we had some breakdowns on special teams, and too many penalties.

On paper, the two teams looked pretty even. The Eagles' offense averaged 470 yards a game, good for fourth place in FCS ratings. The Mountaineers came in a close fifth place, with one yard less. Both teams had athletic quarterbacks who could throw or run. Armanti Edwards' speed and running skills gave him an edge over the Eagles' Matt Nichols, who was taller and outweighed Edwards by 45 pounds.

The Mountaineers took charge early and enjoyed a 21-7 halftime lead. Edwards led the attack with a touchdown run and touchdown passes to Dexter Jackson and Hans Batichon. Special teams gave up an 82-yard kickoff return that led to the Eagles' only score in the first half. The Mountaineers' defense dug in and prevented another Eagles' score when they forced a fumble and recovered it on their own two-yard line. For a team that hadn't lost a fumble all year, the Eagles lost two in the first half.

In the third quarter, Eastern Washington pulled closer on the Mountaineers' special teams' poor play. The Eagles scored two touchdowns on a 78-yard kickoff return and a 51-yard fake punt. Corey Lynch, who held the team record for blocked kicks, chased the runner down and hit him with such force on the goal line that it carried them into the end zone. Lynch was furious at himself and the poor play of the defense.

The Mountaineers answered with a field goal by Julian Rauch and a touchdown run by Devon Moore, who was substituted for an injured Kevin Richardson. With their team leading 31-21 going into the final quarter, fans in Brewer Stadium felt comfortable for the first time.

All-Conference tailback Richardson saw limited action while resting his injured ankle, but he managed to add 69 yards and a touchdown to increase his league-leading touchdown total to 61. Richardson's score capped the afternoon's scoring for the Mountaineers, who finally had taken control of the game at 38-21.

Eastern Washington hadn't given up though. They added two quick scores in the last three minutes, the last one with only 28 seconds left in the game to go home with a respectable 38-35 loss.

The Eagles tried an onside kick out of desperation. But the

Mountaineers swarmed the ball to run out the clock. Statistically, the Mountaineers outgained Eastern Washington 529 yards to 368, well below the Eagles' 463-yard average.

If there can ever be a coined expression in football like the triple-double in basketball or a baseball triple play, All-American Corey Lynch achieved it that Saturday. Lynch intercepted a pass, recovered a fumble, and blocked a field goal. Not a bad afternoon for the outstanding defensive triple-threat senior. Lynch's exploits were acknowledged by students in the stands who were waving a large sign at the TV cameras that read, "You've Just Been Lynched." The sign appeared at The Rock all season in tribute to the talented All-American four-year starter at safety, who would be sorely missed the next year.

Semifinal—Richmond at The Rock

Jerry: *We had some distractions before the Richmond game. We were scheduled to play on ESPN-TV on Saturday at noon, but* [the game] *got switched to Friday night. It was a fair move after Delaware got weathered-in a couple of extra days after their game out in Iowa.*

It didn't matter too much; we made the best of the time we had. The main thing we had to do was to get our special teams concentrating again. They were awful in the James Madison game and against Eastern Washington. Extra points were blocked and field goals rushed and too many touchdowns were given up off punt and kickoff returns. When that happens, it's just one thing: lack of concentration.

There were people in place where they should have been, but they weren't tackling. We had to make some adjustments in our kick coverage before we played Richmond. You can't make mistakes like we made and win games. We were lucky. Our offense picked up the slack by scoring 38 points.

When Richmond came up the mountains to Boone, both teams had identical 11-2 records. The Spiders were members of the tough Colonial Athletic Association, where they were co-champions. The biggest difference was that they had a 21-10 win over Wofford a week before in the quarterfinals, the same team that beat the Mountaineers 42-31 earlier in the season.

It was an unusually mild December day for Boone, but the temperature started falling at sunset and was down near freezing by kickoff time at eight o'clock. The night game generated a lot of excitement for the 24,140 fans that packed Kidd Brewer Stadium. The first two play-off games saw attendance dip to a little over 12,000, partly because students didn't get tickets to the play-off games in their tuition package. Being on ESPN-TV took away some fans that would have otherwise traveled a long distance to see the games.

But this was the semifinals and the Mountaineers were playing at home for the last time, win or lose. Home-field advantage for the third straight year in the play-offs was another school record. And the night game had everybody pumped up. A Friday night game proved to be just the ticket for exam-weary students as they turned out in large numbers. Tailgaters, who filled the parking lot around the stadium and off-campus hotel parking lots, started early. A five o'clock campus rule for beginning tailgate celebrations was ignored and revelers could be found setting up their grills and chairs for a big party as early as three o'clock.

A mouth-watering aroma of barbecued ribs and burgers from hundreds of grills attacked the taste buds of fans as they filtered through the maze of cars to reach Kidd Brewer Stadium. Two hours before game time boom boxes blared the song "We Are the Champions," a 1977 hit by Freddie Mercury and his band, Queen. It had been popular on Appalachian State's campus since the 2005 championship win and could always be heard blaring at top volume among pregame tailgaters.

Mountaineer fans felt the song defined their team. They truly believed their Mountaineers were destined to go back to Chattanooga for a third straight year.

When the crucial contest got under way, the Kidd Brewer stands were rocking with excitement. The high-octane Mountaineers entered the game with a 42-point scoring average and two league-leading offensive stars in Armanti Edwards and Kevin Richardson. On defense, All-American safety Corey Lynch and company were on the prowl to stop the celebrated Spider ground game.

All the hype and big talk were over. Appalachian received the opening kickoff and went to work. It could have been called the Armanti Edwards show. The fleet-footed, wiry quarterback put on a dazzling performance unmatched in FCS football, or any division, for that matter. Edwards ran for two touchdowns and passed for another to speedster Dexter Jackson for a first quarter lead of 21-7. The Spiders were stunned. Jackson's catch and run were a replay of his opening touchdown against Michigan, good for 52 yards.

The Mountaineers didn't let up as Edwards darted through huge holes led by monster tackle and pro prospect Scott Suttle. By halftime, Edwards' total had doubled to four scores and Appalachian carried a 35-21 lead to the locker room.

All during the wild first half, Chancellor Peacock had been cruising up and down in front of the packed ASU side of Kidd Brewer, holding up the two championship trophies. Smiling and wearing a black-and-gold jersey, the chancellor brought thunderous cheers from the student section, where large "Three-Peat" and "You've Just Been Lynched" signs were waved by celebrating students. There was fear that Yosef would run out of ammunition at the rate Armanti and the Mountaineers were scoring. Things calmed down in the third quarter, however.

The Spiders scored one of their touchdowns in the second quarter as a gift from the overzealous Mountaineers. Edwards tacked a somersault dive into the end zone onto his 36-yard touchdown run that drew a flag and a 15-yard penalty on the following kickoff.

Then a very strange series of events unfolded. The first kick by the usually dependable Julian Rauch, who put most of his kickoffs in the end zone, hooked to the left and went out of bounds. A five-yard penalty was assessed on the rekick.

His second kick sliced to the right and went out of bounds again, bringing out more yellow handkerchiefs and another penalty. The striped shirts moved the ball back yet another five yards. On his third try, from the Mountaineers' five-yard line, Rauch sent the ball end over end straight down the middle of the field, where Richmond received it near their own 40-yard line. After the return, the Spiders set up shop on the Mountaineers' 35-yard line. With his receivers covered, quarterback Eric Ward scrambled to elude the black-and-gold rush and found an opening for the score with only 21 seconds left in the half.

*Photograph by Mark Mitchell/*Watauga Democrat

Appalachian State University chancellor Dr. Kenneth Peacock leads student body cheers while waving two national championship trophies during a 2007 play-off game.

Their last-second score before the half fired the Spiders up. They came out after the break and scored on their first possession. CoCo Hillary had the ball stripped inside the Mountaineers' 30-yard line on the ensuing kickoff. A few plays later, Ward again had to scramble to find an opening to dodge his way into the Mountaineers' end zone from five yards out.

Richmond's two quick third-quarter touchdowns quieted the Appalachian side of The Rock and tied the game at 35-35. If the crowd was deflated, the Mountaineers weren't. Immediately, with their next possession, the Mountaineers took control again and marched down the field with ease. Richardson made his statement with touchdown No. 18 on the season.

Appalachian's defense decided they had had enough of the Spiders and shut them down in the final quarter. The last period turned into the Nic Cardwell show, accompanied by Armanti Edwards. The 230-pound senior tight end scored on two of Edwards' 14 pass completions to bury Richmond 55-35.

> Jerry: *I was really proud to see Nic make those two catches. He's a walk-on who's really worked hard. He worked through a shoulder injury so bad that the doctors told him not to play anymore. He worked extra hard in rehab and has been a real contributor to our team. He really deserved those touchdowns. I think that doubled his career total. It was great for a senior's last home game.*

The celebration was on as Appalachian students flooded the field and began their regular ritual of taking down one of the goalposts. A wise administration installed removable goalposts years earlier so the students could celebrate without destroying expensive equipment. Earlier in the season, the students expressed their gratitude when they paraded around campus and placed the goalpost on Chancellor Peacock's lawn after the historic win over Michigan.

> Jerry: *During the Richmond game, I looked back and was amazed at the huge crowd and the loud spirit they showed throughout the game. It set a record for a play-off game. We have held the conference attendance record for several years now. That speaks volumes about our program and school.*

Our students are awesome with their support. They really get into it with the body paint, signs, and stuff like that. I really like the signs they come up with, like the ones they wave after Corey makes a tackle or intercepts a pass or recovers a fumble; that's really neat and the players get a big kick out of them. There was a new one that showed up after Armanti had his big game against Richmond. It looked like a Heisman Trophy ballot sheet and his name was checked. That was a neat deal. I think several million people in the TV audience saw just how supportive our students and fans can be. Nobody appreciates them more than our players. The players always salute them after the game in appreciation of their great support.

Our allotment of 7,800 tickets for the championship game sold out before noon on Saturday after we beat Richmond. I think we had more at the game than the year before at Chattanooga. Everyone was really excited about the chance for a three-peat. I promise you, that stadium was packed full of folks dressed in black and gold.

2007 National Championship—Delaware

Jerry: *We were really excited about going back to Chattanooga for a third straight year. We could finally concentrate on the championship game. It wasn't hard to get the players excited. We had kind of put the championship in the back of our minds to concentrate on the team we had to play next in the play-offs, but it was there. I think our guys handled it really well.*

We had a little distraction with one of our best players, and I had to suspend him just before we left for Chattanooga. That's a rough deal. He was a senior and you hate to see a player who has meant so much to the team mess up like that just before his last game, especially a championship game.

Kidd Brewer Stadium's parking lot was full of well-wishers who had come to see the Mountaineers off. A pep rally with a lot of handshaking and backslapping was aimed at the team as they loaded onto the buses for the five-and-a-half-hour trip to Chattanooga. Everybody was accounted for, except star cornerback Justin Woazeah.

"Justin Woazeah won't play in the championship game Friday night," Coach Moore said to the press before boarding the Chattanooga-bound buses. "The team has rules. We all have rules that we live by. Those rules have been in effect for years and we have to adhere to them. What he did wasn't a big deal. But we have rules and we're going to stand by them."

Coach Moore wouldn't say what the infraction was. It was a team matter. As a strict disciplinarian he didn't hesitate to dismiss one of his best defensive players for a team-rule violation. He said it wasn't a big deal, which was interpreted as not serious. But whatever it was, the action violated a team rule. The consequence was dismissal, ending a brilliant career one game short of his third championship game. Justin was a starter his freshman year and played in 54 of 55 games in his four years. He was an all-time conference leader in broken-up passes and was as good a tackler as he was a pass defender.

It was an unfortunate way for the Mountaineers to begin defense of their national championship for the second straight year.

Spirits were high when they reached Chattanooga, where a Super Bowl–like atmosphere engulfed the whole city. There was team-bowling night, media day, and a last-minute walk-through before the crucial game.

Coach Moore was not one to break a lucky tradition. The team watched for the third time the *Miracle on Ice* movie for inspiration. Even though the seniors had already seen it twice before, they still got the message of hope and spirit of fighting against the odds.

The game was hyped in the media as a match of the two FCS titans. Stories abounded about the Blue Hens' quarterback, Joe Flacco, who was projected to go in the early rounds of the NFL draft. His tailback, Omar Cuff, was the leading rusher in the Colonial Athletic Association. The combination could put points on the board quickly, and they finished the season with a 37-points-per-game average. The Blue Hens rolled up 59 points in a win over a nationally ranked Navy team. They lit up the scoreboard with 56 points in a losing effort to James Madison in five overtimes during the regular season.

No slouches themselves, the Mountaineers, at 12-2, averaged 42 points and also had a tandem scoring team of quarterback Armanti Edwards and tailback Kevin Richardson. The two backs were the first Southern Conference players on the same team to rush for over 2,000 yards each. Edwards' rushing record plus his 1,000 passing yards both set conference records. In the semifinal game Edwards broke a conference and team rushing record, racking up 313 yards against James Madison, and he passed for another 182 yards, completing 14 of 16 attempts.

Championship games have brought out the best in teams, and they often defy all the pregame statistics. It's like sudden-death overtime in the NFL. You only get one chance to prove you are the champion. Chattanooga is dwarfed by the crowds at FCS championship bowl games. But when the final whistle blows for those 25,000 fans, the last team standing has earned their crown and the right to be called champions.

The pregame skepticism of the Mountaineers' leaky defense never materialized. Delaware's befuddled defense couldn't stop the

*Photograph by Mark Mitchell/*Watauga Democrat

Kevin Richardson bulls his way toward Delaware's end zone for one of his season-high 21 touchdowns in the 49-21 championship victory.

Mountaineers' offense and the Blue Hens were unable to penetrate the much-maligned Appalachian defense.

Armanti and company came out and scored on their first three possessions. Having read Edwards' statistics of the previous week's game, the Blue Hens concentrated on stopping the shifty runner. That was fine with Armanti, he just pitched or passed it to Richardson who ran it in.

A fired-up defense shut out the Blue Hens, who were accustomed to scoring when they reached the red zone. They thought they had matched Appalachian's first touchdown to even the score when Omar Cuff plunged into the end zone from the five-yard line. The celebration was cut short upon review, which showed Cuff's elbow had touched the ground before the ball broke the goal-line plane.

Another shot at the Mountaineers' goal line by Cuff from inside the one-yard line was stopped by Corey Lynch and Anthony Williams. On fourth and goal, from inches away, quarterback Flacco dropped back to pass. He couldn't find an open receiver and retreated back beyond the 20-yard line to escape three Mountaineers in pursuit. His desperation pass floated over the head of his covered receiver in the end zone.

Edwards and company took over on their two-foot line and proceeded down the field for a 99-plus-yard record-setting drive for a touchdown. Trailing 21-0, the Blue Hens squandered a second scoring opportunity when their usually reliable kicker pushed a 35-yard effort wide right.

Coach K. C. Keeler was distraught with the way his team was playing. A sideline huddle with his team paid off. Delaware finally scored on a Flacco pass with 1:10 left in the half. Elated Blue Hens bumped their chests against each other celebrating their comeback.

The celebration was short-lived. It took Armanti Edwards only 26 seconds to find Dexter Jackson open on a short sideline route. Jackson spun away from his defender, reversed direction across the field, and raced down the right sideline for a 60-yard touchdown. Shoulders sagged as all the air went out of the Blue Hens'. A celebrating Appalachian team high-fived their way to the locker room with a 28-7 lead.

Delaware regained a little of their first-touchdown momentum and put up another score to begin the second half. Edwards came right back to open the lead 35-14 with a second touchdown strike to

Richardson. The Mountaineers' defense continued to put pressure on Flacco. The Blue Hens were forced out of their game plan and tried to play catch-up with their highly touted passing game. Flacco was sacked four times, and when he did manage to get a pass off it was knocked down by the inspired Mountaineer pass defense led by Corey Lynch.

The game was winding down to less than four minutes. With a 42-14 lead, the Mountaineers had assured themselves of a third championship. Coach Moore started substituting reserves. He sent senior backup quarterback Trey Elder in for mop-up operations in his last game. And mop up he did.

On his first play, he faked a handoff into the line and dashed around right end untouched for a 53-yard touchdown, the longest of his four-year career. The celebration after that electrifying run brought the whole Appalachian team and Coach Moore running down the field to congratulate him. Moore gave him a big bear hug, watched by millions of TV viewers.

The already charged-up Mountaineer fans took their cue and poured over the rails onto the field below. They crowded right up to the sideline markers on two sides of the field. Some jubilant fans ran out on the field and crowded into the coaches' box. A delay-of-game penalty was called while outmanned security personnel and coaches coaxed the fans off the field.

Order was finally restored and Rauch kicked off for the last time of his outstanding career. The penalty set up a short field for Delaware's return team. Mark Duncan gathered the ball in and streaked through the Mountaineers' kicking team for a 75-yard touchdown.

Duncan's frustration boiled over when he crossed the goal line and threw the ball into a group of Appalachian supporters crowded against the back of the end zone. That just added more excitement for the celebrating black-and-gold fans.

The misery finally ended for Delaware, and the Mountaineer fans lost all their restraint and flooded the field. Jubilant players doused Coach Moore with the traditional Gatorade shower. Fans and players swarmed around the drenched Jerry Moore to express their congratulations. The cold Tennessee night air didn't seem to bother him as he congratulated his players and hugged his seniors for the last time.

In the press conference after the game, 10 starting seniors were still pinching themselves to make sure it wasn't all a dream.

*Photograph by Mark Mitchell/*Watauga Democrat

Coach Moore and Mountaineer players celebrate winning their
third championship in a row after a 49-21 victory over the
University of Delaware.

"Never in my life would I have guessed we would have won three national championships after that 2004 season," said ASU and Southern Conference rushing leader and soon-to-be-named All-American Kevin Richardson.

Nic Cardwell said, "After that season, Coach pulled a group of us together that he felt were leaders and asked us what we needed to change and work on. That's what makes Coach special. He listened to his players."

Touchdown-maker Trey Elder agreed. "That was really a disappointing year for me. I had just come off a perfect 15-0 high-school season and wasn't used to losing that many games. Credit our coaches, they got us to buy into a new system, and it has paid off for us."

"We had more talent than people gave us credit for that year," defensive All-American Kerry Brown said. "We were young at some spots and had some chemistry problems that needed addressing. Coach handled that and we all got together and worked hard as a team and here we are—three-peat national champions. It's a great way to go out as a senior."

All-Southern Conference center Scott Suttle summed it up best: "What happened in 2004 made our team what it is. We went through some real rough times that year. I think we were determined to never go through that again."

> Jerry: *This team is special, especially the seniors. They came out of a disappointing season and a lot of turmoil around here in 2004. I wasn't sure I'd still be the coach. The athletic director was reassigned and a new chancellor came in. It wasn't a fun time to be around, but they pulled it together and won a national championship the next year and the next year and the next year.*
>
> *I couldn't be more pleased for these seniors. They're the ones that made it all happen. I've been at Nebraska and Arkansas with major college football programs, and I don't believe we ever got as much national attention as our football team has here at Appalachian State.*
>
> *These seniors have won three national championships; nobody has done that at this level. That's really special and I couldn't be happier for them.*

EPILOGUE—LIFE AT THE TOP OF THE MOUNTAIN

"Hello, Coach, this is Dick. We need to get together for a final wrap-up of the book. Do you think you can squeeze me in this evening? How's the weather up there?"

"Sure. We had some snow last night and this morning, but the roads are clear. I've got to tie up a couple of loose ends, but I'll be finished up by the time you get to Boone. Margaret's here with me. There are too many distractions here; we can go to the house and finish up. Why don't you meet us here at my office? You can follow us to the house, but stay close; it gets pretty dark out there once you get off the main road. We don't have streetlights."

"Sounds like a good plan to me, see you about six o'clock."

I couldn't believe we had that same conversation three years ago when this odyssey began. I hung up the phone and leaned back in my desk chair. My mind drifted back to our initial meeting in Wilkesboro when I pitched my idea for a book. Coach Moore didn't really believe I would follow through. More than once in the early stages he said, "If you don't want to go through with this, it's okay; you won't hurt my feelings." I followed him around and bugged him with early morning phone calls at his office and late calls at home for three seasons. He finally believed I was serious.

⚬

The sky was as black as ink by the time we turned off U.S. 321. Coach had invited me to follow him home to conduct our final interview. He had told me to stay close. He wasn't kidding. It was dark on those meandering little roads that snaked their way through communities on every hillside. We wove our way back through the unlighted streets under threatening snow clouds that hovered overhead, blocking the stars and moonlight. I heeded Jerry's advice and stayed close. Their taillights were all I could see.

All of a sudden, their taillights disappeared. They suddenly turned off Rembrandt Road. The driveway dropped at a 45-degree angle as I made a blind turn to follow them. It was the same sensation I got when riding a roller coaster that suddenly nosed down one of those steep inclines and brought my stomach up to my throat.

Their house was nestled back in the trees on the side of the mountain below road level. At the bottom of the driveway, house lights cut through the night to guide us inside. Before leaving my car, I glanced at my thermometer. It read 28 degrees. Not a good sign. The temperature was falling and those clouds looked like they could start dropping the white stuff any minute.

Once my eyes adjusted to the darkness, the frozen white blanket of snow highlighted the single-story house they had called home for 17 years. We entered through the double garage that looked more like a storage room. Inside, we navigated the hallway past the kitchen to the living room. An aroma of a fireplace whose logs were now only dead ashes greeted us.

"Regular or decaf?" Margaret asked.

"Decaf for me," I answered, rubbing my hands together briskly to get the blood moving again.

"You two go on in and make yourselves comfortable. Jerry, why don't you build a fire to knock the chill off?"

I checked out all the blankets, pillows, plates, and other Appalachian State paraphernalia that adorned the room while Jerry stacked the wood and lit a fire with the help of a starter log. Soon a fire was popping and crackling in the beautiful floor-to-ceiling stone fireplace.

Margaret served our steaming coffee. I wrapped my hands around the cup. With my first swallow I felt it warming me up on the inside as the heat from the fireplace crept toward us. We hunkered down on a semicircle of couches and chairs that faced the roaring fire. I was finally warm and comfortable—now back to work. My recorder blinked at me, a warning that its batteries were getting low, so we finished our conversation off the record, so to speak.

"Coach, you've been at the top of your profession three years in a row. What's it like to be king of the mountain?"

"Well, I don't know if I really think of it like that. We really don't get to stop and think about that a lot. If you do that you won't win many more of them. I mean I enjoy the day-to-day things that happen, but I really enjoy getting ready for next year. Just like we spent several hours today talking about the off-season workout that will start at six o'clock next Monday morning. I don't really relish what happened the last two or three years too long. There's too much to do to get ready for next season for that."

"Is this the calm after the storm, before you hit the recruiting trail again?"

"Yeah, this is kind of a dead week before the coaches' convention in Anaheim next week. When we get back we'll hit the road real heavy. The play-offs put us way behind. We have some really good players that were four-year starters graduating this spring. Our backups were rotated in a lot and will be able to step up, but you can never have too many good athletes in this league." Jerry strolled in his Texas gait across the room to punch up the fire some more. He reminded me of John Wayne.

"There really isn't any calm after the storm, especially after the three seasons we have just experienced," Margaret said. "There will always be higher expectations for Appalachian to continue dominating in football, and that means Jerry being gone on recruiting the next few weeks."

"What about you, Margaret? What has helped you the most through your journey with Jerry to the top of the mountain?"

"My quiet time reading my Bible each morning sustains me and prepares me for the rest of the day. When I look back at 46 years as a coach's wife, I know I couldn't have done it without God's help.

"Jerry and I have always led Christian lives since we first met back in college. When he took his first coaching job, I wasn't prepared to be a coach's wife. But I loved him. He was the man I wanted to spend the rest of my life with, so I learned how to cope with being a coach's wife from Rosemary Acree, back in Corsicana. That's where Jerry had his first coaching job. She was Coach Acree's wife and was a lifesaver for me.

"It's been a great ride, though, especially these last three years. I wouldn't change a thing, even when there were bad times. I used my morning Bible study for reassurance and spiritual guidance. Psalms always seemed to have just the right verses for me.

"It started with the big win over Georgia Southern in 2005 after we had a disappointing loss to Furman the week before. There had been a lot of turmoil and adversity aimed towards Jerry after the 2004 season and it continued into the beginning of the 2005. This passage just blew me away. Psalm 21, verses 8–13: 'Your hand will lay hold on all your enemies. Though they plot evil against you and devise wicked schemes, they cannot succeed. Be exalted, O Lord, in your strength; we will sing and praise your might.'

"Every year I found scripture that applied to the season. I get cold chills going back and reading them occasionally. They were scriptures from a Bible-study guide or a random selection, but they were always so appropriate for that time. The Citadel selection was really great. It was Psalm 18, verse 29: 'With your help I can advance against troops; with my God I can scale a wall.' That was so great; we beat the Citadel troops 42-14!

"One of the most meaningful passages in our lives was Psalm 107, verses 4-6: 'Some wandered in desert wastelands, finding no way to a city where they could settle. Then they cried out to the Lord in their trouble, and He delivered them from their distress.' I thought that was so perfect for our time spent in Lubbock.

"Then verses 7-9 answered our prayers when we came to Boone: 'He led them by a straight way to a city where they could settle. Let them give thanks to the Lord for His unfailing love and His wonderful deeds for men, for He satisfied the thirsty and fills the hungry with good things.'

"I could sit here all night and give you scripture passages for almost every game and situation for the last three years. Our faith is our strength and has led us to the greatest years of our lives; it just doesn't get any better than this."

Jerry had slipped back into the kitchen and brought out the coffeepot for refills. He had done most of the talking in the earlier interviews about the football side of their life, so he quietly sipped his black coffee and fixed his gaze on Margaret.

They were still warmly affectionate after 48 years of marriage. Her passionate congratulatory sideline kiss in the closing minutes of the 2007 championship game was caught by a photographer. It was prominently displayed on the front page of the sports section in the *Winston-Salem Journal*. The candid photo spoke volumes of their relationship.

"Margaret, have you seen any change in Coach over the last three years?" I asked.

"No changes at all," she replied. "He is the same around the house as he always was. He's still in great demand as a speaker; he must do 100 a year. He said he was going to cut back on his speaking engagements this year." She aimed a big smile in his direction. "But I haven't seen much change there either. The only time he has turned someone down is when he already had something scheduled."

"Any thoughts about retirement, Coach?"

"Oh, no, if I was going to do that I would have been gone the last two years. I still enjoy it too much. I'll keep doing this as long as I enjoy it and am helping the team and school."

"Coach, I have to ask. What movie did the team watch before the Delaware game?"

"The same one we watched the last two years—*Miracle on Ice*. It's a great motivational film about giving your all and winning against great odds. I think it helps our players get up for the game the next day."

"Let's go back for a minute to the months following the 2004 season. Things got pretty ugly around here; the athletic director was reassigned to another position and the chancellor left. How did you manage to hang on to your job?"

"Well, I didn't get involved in all that stuff. I did the best job I could running our football program. There was a lot of stuff going on, like you said. A lot of it was personal, but our staff handled it well and everything turned out okay for us."

"You came out of that looking pretty good when you won the conference championship and your first national championship in 2005. How did you turn it around so fast?"

"We had good players in 2004 and the year before, too. We were probably one of the best 7-4 and 6-5 teams in the country; we just didn't get in the play-offs. If we had made it to the play-offs, we would have done pretty well, I think. We were just getting better all the time and Richie was playing really well.

"That was the first year we had run the spread offense and it was a learning season for the coaches as well as the players. When we played Wyoming in our first game we didn't play very well, but we improved quite a bit in just one week's time and beat a good Eastern Kentucky team 49-21. From that point on we knew more about what we were doing."

"Most coaches with your record would have moved on up to a Division I FBS program. You have had opportunities to move to bigger programs but stayed at Appalachian. Would you be tempted now if, say, a Big 10 or Big 12 or even an ACC school made you one of those multimillion dollar offers?"

"I don't think anybody could say they wouldn't be interested. It would be hard to say you wouldn't take it, because you don't know. A lot would depend on it being the right situation. They may offer you a lot of money, but it may not be where you want to live. I've had some calls earlier in my career at Appalachian, but I haven't seen a job or place I would rather be than where I am now."

"It must be contagious. Your coaching staff averages nine years at Appalachian. Some have had offers from major Division I FBS programs like Kansas but stayed here. What's your secret?"

"We're all pretty close. We intermix well and have great respect for each other. You hear the term *family* used a lot, well, we really are a family. On Sunday nights our staff always eats dinner together and we've been doing it for the last 19 years. It's just one of those things. There's a lot more to it than going out and making a lot more money at another school. Boone is a nice place to live. Most of our coaches have young children and it's just a neat place to raise a family."

"Coach, you've come full circle since those days in Lubbock when your family sort of scattered out. You have most of your family back with you now. Do you feel like you have proven to the football world that without question, you are a winner?"

"Well, I've often said sometimes you have to suffer adversity to move ahead. We turned it over to God and let Him work. We came through it stronger and I'm a better father, husband, and coach. It has been a team effort at home as well as on the football field."

"We love having Elizabeth and her two children, Trey and Kennedy, living here with us," Margaret said. "Jerry gets to go watch Trey play junior high football, and I pick them up from school, so it works out really great. We get a lot of quality family time.

"Of course, Jerry sees Chris every day at work, and says he's become a pretty good coach. His wife, Tracy, has a teenage daughter from a previous marriage who we love very much. We get to see Chris' daughter by his first marriage when she comes up for the summer. Both daughters are seniors, and they get along real well.

"The only one missing is our oldest son, Scott, who is an emergency-room doctor in Antigo, Wisconsin. He and his wife, Kerry, have two preteen daughters, Jamie and Jackie. They came to all the championship games, and we had an early Christmas with them. They try to come down for at least one game during the season. It's always hard to say goodbye when they leave."

Margaret continued, "Our life is great; I don't think it could get any better. We are happy here and feel loved, especially by our church. They would love us just as much if we hadn't won, that's just the kind of people they are."

"Coach, when you came to Boone on such short notice, did you ever think you would still be here 20 years later?

"Oh, no. Probably not until after the '95 season [the first undefeated regular season] did we feel like we were settled in. From '95 on through now, we helped the same guys that were playing for us then and now are coaching for us. We kept improving and went to the semifinals in 2000. I guess those were the two big years that solidified our staff."

"Well, Coach, after three championships in a row, do you think you have anything left to prove? How do you like your chances of going back to Chattanooga next year?"

"We haven't thought about that. All we are trying to do now is get them ready for spring practice and get the right guys in the right spot. We only have 15 practices before two-a-days start. If we get them in the right spots then we can get a lot of work done. So we really haven't thought past working them out hard."

"According to the *Winston-Salem Journal* you have some pretty good recruits committed for next season."

"We won't know that until they get here. We think we got some good players. We have some big holes to fill in our defensive secondary; most of them were four-year starters and will graduate this spring. We'll just have to wait and see how things turn out.

"Did you hear we're playing LSU in our first game this fall?"

"No, I hadn't heard. What a great idea, a play-off between the FBS and the FCS championship teams."

"Yeah, I expect there will be a lot of hype about that. We're excited about it. Most of our guys will have the experience of playing a major program at Michigan last year to draw on. We're really looking forward to it."

"You played them pretty well three years ago, but you won't be able to sneak up on them like you did Michigan."

"We'll prepare for them just like we do for every other team on our schedule. It should be a good game. It's good experience for the team to get to play a team at that level, and like Michigan, it will bring a lot of attention to our school and program. We've already seen the benefits of the Michigan game. We probably got a few players we wouldn't have if we hadn't beaten Michigan."

I glanced out the window. "It's snowing again. Guess I better head back to Winston before the roads get bad. Thanks for the coffee and all the time you've so freely given these last three years to pull this remarkable story together. Coach, I have one last question. If there is one thing you want to be remembered for, what would it be?"

"I haven't really thought much about that. I don't think it could be just one thing. I've always tried to be a good example, especially for the young men. I tried to show them the importance of having a good work ethic and trying to do things right on and off the field. I talk to the players a lot about giving everything their best effort. It has always been important to me to be a good husband, father, and coach, in that order."

We left the toasty warmth of the fireplace as I pulled on my coat, hat, and gloves. Jerry and Margaret walked me to the back door. It was an emotional parting. We had become friends and I felt almost like one of their extended family members. I will miss my many visits to Boone. I will miss the camaraderie with Coach Moore and his staff at practice sessions and on the sidelines at game time. I won't miss covering the 6:00 A.M. February conditioning sessions. And I definitely won't miss having to get up at 5:30 in the morning to get Coach Moore's undivided attention for a few minutes on the phone before he starts his workday.

"Oh, I forgot to tell you," Margaret said, "we're going to Bonham next week. Jerry's hometown is honoring him with a Jerry Moore Day celebration. A lot of his old high school friends will be there. We look forward to visiting his mother, who still lives in Bonham. It will be great to see everybody again."

"I think that is so great. You left Texas under a dark cloud of defeat and are returning now as a three-time national champion—King of the Mountain."

It felt like a two-minute drill to get in everything I felt like I wanted to ask. But the clock ran out and it was time to go. A vice-grip handshake from Jerry, a hug from Margaret, and I headed out the door. Halfway to my car, I stopped and turned in the snow for one last goodbye, "It's been great fun. Coach, you know I can put out a revised edition of this book every year. Good luck in 2008. I'll be rooting for you to keep those championships coming."

Photograph by Dick Brown

Margaret and Coach Moore accompanied the three national championship trophies on a statewide Yosef Club tour that shared the unprecedented achievement by the Appalachian State Mountaineer football team with as many fans and boosters as possible.

FOR THE RECORD

Coaching Honors for Coach Moore
◊ American Football Coaches Association National Coach of the Year: 2005, 2006, 2007
◊ Grant Teaff Lifetime Achievement Award (Fellowship of Christian Athletes): 2007
◊ Eddie Robinson Award (National Coach of the Year—The Sports Network): 2006
◊ American Football Coaches Association Regional Coach of the Year: 1991, 1994, 1995, 2005
◊ Southern Conference Coach of the Year: 1991, 1994, 1995, 2005, 2006, 2007

Coach Moore's Achievements
◊ Winningest coach in Southern Conference history: 117-35
◊ Winningest coach in Appalachian State history: 167-70
◊ Career head coaching record: 194-118

Team achievements under Coach Moore in 2007
◊ ASU was the first team to ever win three consecutive NCAA Division I FCS/I-AA championships.

◊ ASU was the first FCS team to ever defeat a nationally ranked FBS opponent (34-32 at No. 5 Michigan).

◊ Appalachian State University football made history when it became the first non-Division I Football Bowl Subdivision (FBS—formerly Division I-A) program to ever receive votes in the season's final Associated Press college football poll. Appalachian received five points in the final 2007 AP poll, good for a tie for 34th.

◊ Appalachian's monumental 34-32 victory at No. 5 Michigan in the 2007 season opener precipitated a change in the AP policy, which previously allowed only FBS programs to be eligible for inclusion in its college football poll. Thanks to the so-called Appalachian State Rule, ASU received 19 points (good for 33rd overall) in its first week of eligibility (September 9) and five points (34th) in voting for the September 16 poll.

◊ The Mountaineers received more points in the final AP poll than 30 teams that participated in bowls and finished tied with South Florida, which was ranked as high as No. 2 in the AP poll during the 2007 campaign.

◊ ASU was Sports' Biggest Newsmaker of the Year (ESPN.com poll).

◊ ASU was Sports' Second-Biggest Newsmaker of the Year (*USA Today* poll).

◊ ASU was a finalist for the Pontiac Game-Changing Performance of the Year (Corey Lynch's field-goal block at Michigan).

◊ ASU won the Pontiac Game-Changing Performance of the Week $5,000 award (Corey Lynch's field goal block at Michigan).

◊ ASU was named National Team of the Week for the September 1 at Michigan (Football Writers Association of America, College Sporting News).

◊ ASU's September game at Michigan was named the College Football Game of the Year, earning $5,000 award (United States Sports Academy).

Individual player awards for 2007

Pierre Banks—linebacker

◊ First-team All-America (The Sports Network)
◊ First-team All-Southern Conference (media)
◊ National Academic All-Star Team (National Association of Collegiant Directors of Athletics)

◊ Academic All-District (College Sports Information Directors of America)

◊ Academic All-Southern Conference

Hans Batichon—wide receiver

◊ Honorable Mention All-America

Kerry Brown—offensive line

◊ National Lineman of the Year (College Sporting News)

◊ First-team All-America (Associated Press, Walter Camp, American Football Coaches Association, The Sports Network, College Sporting News)

◊ Second-team All-America (College Sports Report)

◊ Southern Conference Jacobs Blocking Trophy (Lineman of the Year—coaches)

◊ First-team All-Southern Conference (coaches and media)

◊ Texas vs. The Nation All-Star Bowl participant

Brad Coley—offensive tackle

◊ Second-team All-Conference (coaches)

Armanti Edwards—quarterback

◊ First-team All-America (College Sporting News)

◊ Second-team All-America (The Sports Network)

◊ National Star of the Year (Sports Media Entertainment Network)

◊ NCAA Division I play-offs MVP (College Sporting News)

◊ Second-team All-Southern Conference (coaches)

◊ National Player of the Week for the September 1 at Michigan (Sports Media Entertainment Network)

◊ Southern Conference Offensive Player of the Month (November)

◊ Southern Conference Offensive Player of the Week (September 1 at Michigan; November 3 at The Citadel)

Trey Elder—quarterback

◊ Southern Conference Offensive Player of the Week (September 8 vs. Lenoir-Rhyne)

Brad Hardee—linebacker

◊ Academic All-Southern Conference

John Holt— offensive guard
◊ Third-team All-America (The Sports Network)
◊ Second-team All-Southern Conference (media)

Dexter Jackson—wide receiver
◊ Honorable Mention All-America (The Sports Network)
◊ Second-team All-Southern Conference (coaches)
◊ Senior Bowl participant
◊ East-West Shrine Game participant

Corey Lynch—safety
◊ Buck Buchanan Award finalist (National Defensive Player of the Year)
◊ National Defensive Player of the Year (College Sporting News)
◊ First-team All-America (Associated Press, Walter Camp, The Sports Network, College Sporting News, College Sports Report—third straight year as All-America)
◊ Southern Conference Defensive Player of the Year (coaches and media)
◊ National Player of the Week for the September 1 at Michigan (The Sports Network, Sports Media Entertainment Network)
◊ Southern Conference Defensive Player of the Month (September)
◊ Southern Conference Defensive Player of the Week (September 1 at Michigan; October 27 vs. Furman)
◊ Texas vs. The Nation All-Star Bowl participant

Julian Rauch—kicker
◊ Second-team All-America (The Sports Network)
◊ First-team All-Southern Conference (coaches and media)

Kevin Richardson—running back
◊ Walter Payton Award finalist (National Player of the Year)
◊ Third-team All-America (The Sports Network)
◊ First-team All-Southern Conference (coaches and media)
◊ Southern Conference Offensive Player of the Week (September 29 at Elon; November 10 at Western Carolina)

Tony Robertson—defensive line
◊ Honorable Mention All-America (The Sports Network)

◊ Second-team All-Southern Conference

Jacque Roman—linebacker
◊ Honorable Mention All-America (The Sports Network)

Cory Rycroft—defensive line
◊ Academic All-Southern Conference

D. J. Smith—linebacker
◊ Honorable Mention All-America (The Sports Network)
◊ Southern Conference Defensive Player of the Month (November)
◊ Southern Conference Defensive Player of the Week (November 17 vs. Chattanooga)

Scott Suttle—center
◊ Third-team All-America (The Sports Network)
◊ First-team All-Southern Conference (coaches and media)

Gary Tharrington—defensive end
◊ Third-team All-America (Associated Press, The Sports Network)
◊ First-team All-Southern Conference (coaches and media)

Jerome Touchstone—defensive back
◊ First-team All-America (College Sporting News)
◊ Third-team All-America (The Sports Network)
◊ First-team All-Southern Conference (coaches)
◊ Second-team All-Southern Conference (media)

Anthony Williams— defensive tackle
◊ First-team All-America (The Sports Network)
◊ Second-team All-Southern Conference (coaches and media)
◊ Southern Conference Defensive Player of the Week (September 15 vs. Northern Arizona)
◊ Academic All-Southern Conference

Russell Wilson—long snapper
◊ Academic All-Southern Conference

Players under Coach Moore who played in the National Football League

1990	Derrick Graham, offensive tackle	Kansas City Chiefs, Carolina Panthers, Seattle Seahawks, Oakland Raiders
	Keith Collins, defensive back	San Diego Chargers
1992	Gary Dandridge, defensive back	Seattle Seahawks
	Mike Frier, defensive tackle	Cincinnati Bengals, Seattle Seahawks
1993	Harold Alexander, punter	Atlanta Falcons
1996	Matt Stevens, defensive back	Buffalo Bills, Philadelphia Eagles, Washington Redskins, New England Patriots, Houston Texans
1997	Dexter Coakley, linebacker	Dallas Cowboys, St. Louis Rams
2001	Corey Hall, defensive back	Atlanta Falcons
	Daniel Wilcox, tight end	New York Jets, Baltimore Ravens, Tampa Bay Buccaneers
2002	Justin Seaverns, linebacker	Miami Dolphins
2005	Jason Hunter, defensive end	Green Bay Packers
2006	Marques Murrell, defensive end	Philadelphia Eagles

2007	Corey Lynch, free safety	Cincinnati Bengals
	Dexter Jackson, wide receiver	Tampa Bay Buccaneers
	Kerry Brown, offensive line	Washington Redskins, free agent
	Julian Rauch, kicker	Pittsburgh Steelers, free agent

Players under Coach Moore who played in the Canadian Football League

2004	Wayne Smith, offensive tackle	Saskatchewan Roughriders
2006	Richie Williams, quarterback	Hamilton Tiger Cats

ACKNOWLEDGMENTS

I would like to thank the people and recognize the resources that contributed to this book. Without them, I couldn't have gathered the necessary information and assembled it into the story of Coach Jerry Moore and the Appalachian State football team.

Appalachian State University Library
Appalachian State University Athletic Department
Head Coach Jerry Moore and his wife, Margaret Moore
Coach Moore's assistant coaches
Charlie Cobb, athletic director
Mike Flynn, asst. athletic director/sports information
David Jackson, ISP Sports Network "Voice of the Mountaineers", and his father Randy Jackson who covered the sideline action of the Mountaineers
Chattanooga Times Free Press photo editor Billy Weeks
Waco-McLennan County Library
Watauga Democrat sports editor Steve Behr

Photographers Mark Mitchell, Marie Freeman, Bill Sheffield, and Rob Moore
Winston-Salem Journal
Billy Graham Evangelistic Association

Last but certainly not least, my thanks go to Carolyn Sakowski and designer Angela Harwood whose dedication on a very short deadline made this book come alive.

NOTES FROM THE AUTHOR

I've been told this book was either a timely accident or a quirk of fate. I prefer to think it was a little of both.

The last seven years we lived in Texas, after I took early retirement from Raytheon as a publications/graphics supervisor for Proposal Services, I worked as a journalist for a series of newspapers—first for the twice-weekly *Commerce Journal*, then the Greenville *Herald Banner*, a daily paper. In addition to my regular reporting duties, I had to cover a football game every week out in the county. It was hard work, but I really enjoyed it and always looked forward to the fall football season. I also wrote a column called "The Bottom Line," which I continued in the *Bay City Tribune*, when we moved to Bay City after I retired as a full-time journalist from the *Herald Banner*. It was fun and easy because many of the columns were about my grandchildren and the goings-on in the city of Greenville and the little town of Bay City, Texas.

I had to give up the column when we moved back to North Carolina. I was disappointed the *Winston-Salem Journal* didn't pick up my column. But that turned out to be a good thing. It gave me time to do some serious writing. The writing juices were still flowing, so I turned back to an old unfinished manuscript taking up space on my computer hard drive. I read it over and realized why I never finished it. I needed something new and fresh.

About that time the North Carolina legislature was discussing raising the cigarette tax. The state needed the revenue and thought it might slow down the illegal trafficking of cigarettes. Then a light went on in my head. What a perfect vehicle for a novel—the illegal bootlegging of cigarettes from North Carolina to New York. I started my research and outlined a few chapters, laying groundwork for my great American novel.

In the meantime I became a big fan of the Appalachian State Mountaineers and Coach Jerry Moore, whom I had known while he was coaching at Texas Tech. As the Mountaineers picked up momentum, rolling up wins with big scores in the 2005 season, work on the cigarette-bootlegging novel stopped. My fascination with Appalachian State grew and I began reading everything I could find on the Mountaineers and Coach Moore. The 2002 "Mountaineer Miracle" game against Furman really caught my attention. That would make a great story, I thought. Was there enough for a book based on that one game? The more I read, the bigger the story got. *Magic on the Mountain* was my working title, and I started writing.

I contacted Coach Moore, and we met in Wilkesboro. I pitched my idea of a book about him and his football team. He agreed to make himself available. That conversation was the beginning of a three-year odyssey. A series of interviews followed and the story grew beyond football. One day after we had finished an interview, we started talking about Texas. He leaned back, got that faraway look in his eyes, and started talking about Bonham and his life there. We kept talking, and Appalachian State kept winning.

The Mountaineers gave me the perfect ending by winning their first national championship in the 2005 season. What a way to end the story! I had written the conclusion midway through the 2006 season. You know what happened next. They won a second national title. I did a rewrite to include the ASU record back-to-back championships. Confident that was the end, I began thinking how I was going to get my book published before the 2007 season.

Then the Michigan game happened the first week of the 2007 season. That monster win had to be included, even if they didn't win another game all season. But they did win more games. They won their third straight Southern Conference Championship and unprecedented third consecutive national championship.

I had to go back and rewrite the ending a third time to include their three-peat championship. I couldn't believe that what started out as a book inspired by a single game had morphed into an incredible three-season saga of Mountaineer magic, plus the wonderful saga of a little kid from Bonham, Texas, who is sitting on top of the football world as the winningest coach in the Southern Conference, and the story of the only Division I FCS team to win three consecutive national championships. Trying to write and publish this book in almost real time has been a phenomenal journey that I have truly enjoyed. What was first called *Magic on the Mountain* had now become a story of a man who rose from the plains of Texas to become King of the Mountain in North Carolina.

Sitting in Coach Moore's office several weeks after the Delaware win for their third championship, I said, "Coach, you've got to stop winning the championship every year, or I'll never finish the book."

He looked across his desk, covered with papers, magazines, and a stack of game tapes, and said with a big grin, "Well, I guess that's your problem, isn't it?"

BIOGRAPHY

Dick Brown was born and raised in Spencer, North Carolina. His first attempt at writing was as a 10-year-old after seeing a movie about dinosaurs on a lost continent, many years before *Jurassic Park*. Those stories were kept hidden and consequently were lost over the years. His first byline came as a member of the *Spencer High Life* newspaper staff.

During his 27-year career as a graphic artist and supervisor of a graphic publications group for Raytheon, he earned a degree in journalism from Texas A&M University–Commerce. Dick worked as a journalist for the *Commerce Journal* (Commerce, Texas), the *Herald Banner* (Greenville, Texas), and the *Bay City Tribune* (Bay City, Texas).

He and his wife, Penny, moved to Winston-Salem, North Carolina, after his retirement as a journalist. He was inspired to try his hand at writing a novel after winning third place in a Winston-Salem short-story-writing contest. He put that idea on hold to write *King of the Mountain*, a creative nonfiction book, after reacquainting himself with Coach Jerry Moore nearly 20 years after Moore was fired by Texas Tech.

Dick resides in Winston-Salem with his wife, Penny, who is an artist in the medium of bead-weaving. Their three children and four grandchildren live in Texas, California, and Washington, D.C.

Index